Advance Praise for Amy James's Knowledge Essentials Series

"Knowledge Essentials is a remarkable series that will _____ abilities and learning styles. Amy James has taken a cl_____ standards and testing around the country and develop_____ ative activities that support what's being taught at each _____, while remaining sensitive to the fact that children learn at different rates and in different ways. I highly recommend it for all parents who want to make a difference in their children's education."

> —Michael Gurian, author of *Boys and Girls Learn Differently*
> and *The Wonder of Boys*

"Finally, a book about teaching young children by somebody who knows her stuff! I can (and will) wholeheartedly recommend this series to the ever-growing number of parents who ask me for advice about how they can help their children succeed in elementary school."

> —LouAnne Johnson, author of *Dangerous Minds*
> and *The Queen of Education*

"Having examined state standards nationwide, Amy James has created innovative and unique games and exercises to help children absorb what they *have* to learn, in ways that will help them *want* to learn. Individualized to the child's own learning style, this is a must-have series for parents who want to maximize their child's ability to succeed in and out of the classroom."

> —Myrna B. Shure, Ph.D., author of *Thinking Parent, Thinking Child*

"The books in Amy James's timely and unique Knowledge Essentials series give parents a clear idea of what their children are learning and provide the tools they need to help their children live up to their full academic potential. This is must reading for any parent with a school-age child."

> —Michele Borba, Ed.D., author of *Nobody Likes Me,*
> *Everybody Hates Me* and *No More Misbehavin'*

FOURTH GRADE SUCCESS

Knowledge Essentials®

*First Grade Success: Everything You Need to Know
to Help Your Child Learn*

*Second Grade Success: Everything You Need
to Know to Help Your Child Learn*

*Third Grade Success: Everything You Need
to Know to Help Your Child Learn*

*Fourth Grade Success: Everything You Need
to Know to Help Your Child Learn*

FOURTH GRADE SUCCESS

Everything You Need to Know to Help Your Child Learn

AMY JAMES

JOSSEY-BASS
A Wiley Imprint
www.josseybass.com

Published by Jossey-Bass
A Wiley Imprint
989 Market Street, San Francisco, CA 94103-1741

Design and composition by Navta Associates, Inc.

Jossey-Bass books and products are available through most bookstores. To contact Jossey-Bass directly call our Customer Care Department within the U.S. at 800-956-7739, outside the U.S. at 317-572-3986, or fax 317-572-4002.

Jossey-Bass also publishes its books in a variety of electronic formats. Some content that appears in print may not be available in electronic books.

Library of Congress Cataloging-in-Publication Data:

James, Amy, date.
    Fourth grade success : everything you need to know to help your child learn / Amy James.
        p. cm. — (Knowledge essentials)
    Includes bibliographical references and index.
    ISBN-13 978-0-471-46819-6 (pbk.)
    ISBN-10 0-471-46819-3 (pbk.)
    1. Fourth grade (Education) 2. Fourth grade (Education)—Curricula—United States.
3. Education, Elementary—Parent participation.   I. Title.   II. Series.
    LB15714th .J36 2005
    372.24'1—dc22   2005004699

Printed in the United States of America

FIRST EDITION

PB Printing 10 9 8 7 6 5 4 3 2 1

To my granny, Dorothy Cowan

CONTENTS

ACKNOWLEDGMENTS

I would like to thank the following people for advising me on this book:

My mother, Cindy King, is a retired early childhood and reading specialist who taught kindergarten and first grade for thirty years. She assisted in establishing the transition program at her school district for children who are developmentally young.

My father, E. W. James, was an elementary school principal and elementary school teacher for fifteen years. He led the school district's efforts to serve children with special needs.

Gloria Hamlin, my supervising administrator during my teaching years, retired from Norman Public School after spending twenty-two years teaching math and eleven years as a middle school administrator. She directed the math, science, and technology departments.

Elizabeth Hecox is in her sixteenth year of teaching at Kennedy Elementary School in Norman, Oklahoma. She is an incredible classroom teacher, and the book is better because of her work with me on it.

Kim Lindsay is in her twelfth year of teaching elementary school in Dallas Public Schools and in Norman Public Schools. She was elected teacher of the year at Kennedy Elementary School for 2001–2002.

Holly Sharp taught English language arts for thirty years in five states and served as department chair for twelve years. She has written curriculum for Norman Public Schools and is an advisory board member for both the University of Oklahoma and Norman Public Schools.

The employees of Six Things, Inc., are a group of more than twenty current and former teachers who provide invaluable assistance on a daily basis. Anytime I needed help in any subject area, for any grade, their enormously good brains were at my disposal. This book series would not be possible without their assistance, and I am eternally grateful to them for their help.

Introduction

Fourth grade probably sounded like the Promised Land when your child was three, didn't it? Reading, writing, and math would all have been covered, and your child would have turned into a little person whom you could hang out with—not a baby, not a rebellious teenager—just a fun little person who can read his or her own menu at a restaurant. But maybe you forgot the cute name we call fourth graders: tweens.

Are the tween years a sign of things to come? As far as school goes, yes. Fourth graders are showing up at the end of the day with real homework, and you will be the most convenient person to ask for help with it. Fourth graders are old hands at standardized tests. They are writing in illegible cursive and can throw down a string of four-syllable words that they actually know the meaning of.

So is your child already too grown up for you to enhance his or her academic achievements? Absolutely not. You and the learning environment you create in your home can accommodate your child's growth and increasing skill levels no matter how sophisticated he or she is. Learning environments are important—whether your child is at school, at home, or in the car; the way you interact with your little learner will influence his or her abilities for a lifetime.

To effectively enhance your child's learning, you need to be constantly and consistently aware of your child's development over the years so that you can come to know his or her particular strengths, shortcomings, and areas of talent and natural inclination. (Be honest with yourself about the last part; not every little girl is a beauty queen and not every little boy is an athlete.) And just because you know one of your children does not mean you know them all. Children's minds differ substantially. Each child is his or her own person with a unique set of abilities. As you gain insight into your children's development, you can easily help them individually strengthen their abilities while also concentrating on areas of difficulty.

Life at home matters. An academically progressive home life is the key to effectively tracking your child's development as well as providing the opportunity to successfully apply knowledge. Creating the environment is about creating the opportunity to learn. The point is to bring the level of content and conversation in your daily life to the level that is in your child's school life. Home, your child's first learning environment, is the primary testing ground for new knowledge and skills.

Getting the Most from This Book

This book is a guide to creating an exceptional learning environment in your home. It contains curricula and skills unique to fourth grade presented in a way that makes it easy to put what you learn into practice immediately. This book serves as a tool to help solve the mystery behind creating a supportive, learning-rich environment in your home that fosters a thinking child's development while enriching his or her curricula. It contains dozens of mini–lesson plans that contain easy-to-use activities designed to help your child meet your state's learning requirements. An environmental learning section in each chapter tells you how to identify learning opportunities in the everyday world.

Chapters 2 through 4 give you some child development information to get you started. Teaching is about knowing the subject area you teach, but moreover it is about knowing the abilities of the students you teach. As a parent you can easily see the milestones your child reaches at an early age (crawling, walking, talking, etc.), but milestones are not always apparent in your six- to nine-year-old. These chapters explain the child development processes that take place during fourth grade, including what thinking milestones your child's brain is capable of and will reach in normal development during this time. In order for you to teach effectively, you will need to account for these developmental milestones in all topics and skills that you introduce.

Teaching is also about recognizing how different people learn and tailoring the way you teach to suit them. You will find out how to recognize different learning styles in chapter 3, which will help you implement the learning activities in the rest of the book.

Chapters 5 through 11 provide general subject area information for the fourth grade curriculum. The curriculum discussed in this book was chosen by reviewing all fifty of the state learning standards, the National Subject Area Association learning standards, the core curriculum materials that many school districts use, and supplemental education products. While there are some discrepancies in curricula from region to region, they are few and far between. Chances are that even if you aren't able to use all of the topical subject area units (such as social studies and science), you will be able to use most of them. Reading, writing, and math are skill-based subjects, particularly in fourth grade, and those skills are chosen according to specific child developmental indicators. It is likely that you will be able to use all of the information in those chapters. Each chapter provides learning activities that you can do at home with your child.

The focus of chapter 12 is understanding the social environment in fourth grade, including how your child interacts with peers and his or her social needs. Chapter 13 discusses how your child will demonstrate that he or she is prepared for fifth grade. The appendixes provide information on products that meet certain fourth grade learning needs.

You won't read this book from cover to cover while lounging on the beach. Hopefully it will be a raggedy, dog-eared, marked-up book that has been thumbed through, spilled on, and referred to throughout the school year. Here are some tips on using this book:

Do

- Use this book as a reference guide throughout your child's fourth grade year.

- Model activities and approaches after the information you find in this book when creating your own supplemental learning activities.

- Modify the information to meet your needs and your child's needs.

Don't

- Complete the activities in this book from beginning to end. Instead, mix and match them appropriately to the curriculum and/or skills your child is learning in school.

- Use this book as a homeschool curriculum. It will help with your homeschooling in the same way it helps parents that don't home-school—it supplements the fourth grade core curriculum.

- Challenge your child's teacher based on information you find here. ("Why isn't my child covering electricity as it said in *Fourth Grade Success*?") Instead, look for the synergy in the information from both sources.

Use this book and its resources as supplemental information to enhance your child's fourth grade curriculum—and let's make it a good year for everyone!

Getting the Most for Your Fourth Grader

1

No parent says, "Oh, mediocre is okay for my child. Please do things halfway; it doesn't matter." Parents want the best for their children. This is not a matter of spending the most money on education or buying the latest educational toy. It is a matter of spending time with your child and expending effort to maximize what he or she is being provided by the school, by the community, and at home.

Getting the Most from Your School System

You wouldn't think twice about getting the most bang for your buck from a hotel, your gym, or a restaurant, and you shouldn't think twice about getting the most from your school system. The school system was designed to serve your needs, and you should take advantage of that.

Public Schools

Part of learning how to manage life as an adult is knowing how to manage interaction with bureaucratic agencies, so it makes sense that part of this learning take place within a kinder, gentler bureaucratic system. This is a good introduction to working within a system that was formed to assist in the development of children's abilities. Schools are also a workplace—with a chain of command—and that is a good induction into the workplace your child will enter as an adult. To further your children's educational experience, you and your children will have the opportunity to meet and work with:

- School personnel: your child's teacher, teacher's aides, specialists, the school counselor, the administrator or principal, and others

- Extracurricular groups: scouts, sports, after-school programs, and community parks and recreation programs

- Parents: of children from your child's class or grade level, school volunteers, and parent–teacher organizations

Participation in your child's education is paramount to his or her success. Active participation doesn't mean that you have to spend hours at the school as a volunteer, but it does include reading all of the communications your school sends either to you directly or home with your child. Also, read the school handbook and drop by your child's school on a regular basis if possible. If you can't stop by, check out the school or class Web site to see what units are being covered, any upcoming events, and so on. Participation means attending school events when you can, going to class parties when possible, and going to parent–teacher conferences. If they are scheduled at a time when you are not available, request a different time. The school administrator or principal usually requires that teachers try to accommodate your schedule.

The single most important thing you can do to get the most out of your local school system is to talk to your child's teacher. Find out what curricula your child will be covering and how you can help facilitate learning. Does the teacher see specific strengths and weaknesses that you can help enhance or bring up to speed? The teacher can help you identify your child's learning style, social skills, problem-solving abilities, and coping mechanisms.

Teachers play a role that extends outside the classroom. Your child's teacher is the perfect person to recommend systemwide and community resources. Teachers know how to find the local scout leaders, tutors, good summer programs, and community resources. Your child's teacher may be able to steer you in the right direction for getting your child on an intramural team. Teachers are truly partners in your child's upbringing.

Your child's teacher cares about your child's well-being. Everyone has heard stories about having a bad teacher or one who was "out to get my child." If that's the way you feel, then it's even more important to have regular conversations with the teacher. Maybe his or her actions or your child's actions are being misunderstood. In any case, your child's teacher is the main source of information about school and the gateway to resources for the year, so find a way to communicate.

If you know there is a problem with the teacher that needs to be taken seriously, try the following:

- Talk to parents with children in the class ahead of your child. They may be able to tell you how the issue was approached by parents the previous year—and they will have lots to tell about their experiences with teachers your child will have next year.

- Talk to your child's principal. This may result in your child being transferred to another class, so make sure you are prepared for that prior to making the appointment. Be willing to work with your child's current teacher prior to transferring your child. The less disruption your fourth grader experiences, the better.

- Talk to your local school administration center to see what the procedures are for transferring to another school. You will likely be required to provide transportation to a school outside of your home district, but if the problem is severe enough, it will be worth it.

No matter what, active participation and communication with your child's school is essential. It empowers you to:

- Accurately monitor your child's progress
- Determine which optional activities would enrich your child's learning experience
- Prepare your child for upcoming events, curricula, and skill introduction
- Share and add to the school learning environment
- Create a complementary learning environment in your home
- Spend time with your child

And just a word about the school secretary: this person knows more about what is going on in that building than anyone else. When I was a teacher, the school secretary always added to my and my students' success. The secretary is a taskmaster, nurse, mom or dad, and generally just a comforting figure in what can sometimes be a really big building. The school secretary always knows what forms to fill out, which teacher is where, what students are absent and why, when the next school event is, and how much candy money you owe for the latest fund-raiser. He or she is a source of lunch money, milk money, extra pencils, bus passes, and the copy machine. Get to know and love your school secretary.

Private Schools

On a micro level, participating in your child's education if she attends a private school isn't much different from participating if she attends a public school. Private schools have access to the same community resources. If you have a special needs child, the private school should work with local education agencies to see that your child gets the appropriate services. Through active communication and participation, you will derive the same benefits as parents whose children attend public school.

On a macro level, private schools are different from public schools. Private schools are governed not by a school board but by an internal system. This can be both easier and harder to navigate. Dealing with private schools is easier because the schools realize that you are paying tuition every month, so frankly they want to please their customers. Dealing with private schools is harder because they aren't accountable to the community for their actions nor are they governed by the same due processes as the public school system. Check out the school's administration hierarchy to see how decisions are made and what roles have been created for parent governance. Also, get to know the school's secretary.

To really be on top of things, it's a good idea to print a copy of your state's learning standards (see chapter 4) and familiarize yourself with the topics and skills that your state thinks fourth graders should learn. You can find a copy at www.knowledgeessentials.com. Compare the standards to those of your private school's fourth grade curriculum. If the curriculum is drastically different from the required state learning standards, your child will have difficulty passing the required state assessments. If your child's curriculum meets and exceeds the standards, your child will be well served by that school.

Private schools have the flexibility to incorporate religious elements or varied teaching philosophies that public schools can't provide. They are not subject to the separation of church and state requirements. Private schools operate without depending on community support (such as bond proposals); so as long as their tuition-paying constituency approves of their methods and the students who graduate from the programs demonstrate success, private schools can implement teaching methods at will that fall out of the mainstream.

Getting the Most from Your Homeschool Curriculum

A little power is a dangerous thing. You are homeschooling your child because you want more control over what and how your child learns and the environment in which he learns it. That is admirable, but don't be fooled. To a large extent, your child's natural ability to learn certain things at certain times will dictate the way you should approach any homeschool curriculum (chapters 2 and 3 explain this more fully). The best thing you can do when starting to homeschool your child is look at books on child development. Start with these:

- *Children's Strategies: Contemporary Views of Cognitive Development*, edited by David F. Bjorklund. Hillsdale, N.J.: Erlbaum Associates, 1990.

- *Piaget's Theory: Prospects and Possibilities*, edited by Harry Beilin. Hillsdale, N.J.: Erlbaum Associates, 1992.

- *Instructional Theories in Action: Lessons Illustrating Selected Theories and Models*, edited by Charles M. Reigeluth. Hillsdale, N.J.: Erlbaum Associates, 1987.

- *All Our Children Learning*, Benjamin S. Bloom. New York: McGraw-Hill, 1981.

You don't have to homeschool your child all by yourself or by limiting yourself to a particular homeschool organization's materials. Each state has some form of a regional education system with centers open to the public. At your public school system's curriculum resource center, you can check out curriculum materials and supplemental materials. Most of these centers have a workroom with things like a die press that cuts out letters and shapes from squares to animals to holiday items. Regional education centers often provide continuing education for teachers, so they usually have some training materials on hand. Look for information about your regional center on your state department of education's Web site. You can find a link to your state department of education at www.knowledgeessentials.com.

You can purchase homeschool curriculum kits designed to provide your child with a lion's share of the materials needed to complete a grade level. You can also buy subject area–specific curricula. It is important to ask the company that sells the curriculum to correlate the materials with your state's learning standards so that you can see which standards you need to reinforce with additional activities. You can find the companies that sell these kits at www.knowledgeessentials.com.

Using Supplemental Materials

You cannot expect any single curriculum in any public school, private school, or homeschool to meet all of the learning standards for the grade level and subject area in your state. Many will meet 90 percent of the standards and some will meet 75 percent, which is why there are supplemental materials. Schools use them and so should you. They are simply extra materials that help your child learn more. Examples of these materials include:

- Trade books. These are just books that are not textbooks or work-books—in other words, the kind of books, fiction and nonfiction, that you would check out at the library or that your child would choose at a bookstore. Trade books don't have to tell about many things in a limited number of pages so they can tell a lot more about a single topic than a textbook can. They give your child a chance to practice skills that she is learning. If you choose wisely, you can find books that use newly learned reading skills, such as compound words, blends, prefixes and suffixes, or rhyming. Sometimes these skills will be set in the context of newly learned science or social studies topics, such as weather, habitats, or your community. Many companies provide these types of books for sale, but the most recognizable one may be Scholastic, Inc. Appendix A lists some books that are really good for fourth graders.

- Software and the Internet. Schools choose electronic activities and content, such as educational software and Internet sites, and electronic components, such as Leapfrog's LeapMat, allowing your child to expand his content knowledge while implementing skills just learned. Supplementing what your child is learning at school with these resources helps him gain technology skills within a familiar context. If you choose wisely, such as starting with the software choices listed in appendix B of this book, you can sometimes enhance reading skills and/or supplement a social studies or science topic while your child learns to operate a computer—talk about bang for your buck.

- Other materials. Videos, photographs, audio recordings, newspapers—just about anything you can find that helps expand what your child is learning is a supplemental resource. Loosely defined, supplemental resources can include a wide array of materials; your newly trained eye is limited only to what you now know is appropriate for your child.

Now you know what we need to cover, so let's get to it.

Fourth Grade Development

2

Good teachers base their activities on the developmental stages at which their students are performing. What is a developmental stage and why is it important?

The ability to learn is always related to your child's stage of intellectual development. Developmental stages describe how a child thinks and learns in different growth periods. These periods are loosely defined by age but are more accurately defined by behavior. They are important because children cannot learn something until physical growth gives them certain abilities; children who are at a certain stage cannot be taught the concepts of a higher stage (Brainerd, 1978).

The theory of child development that is the basis for modern teaching was formed by Jean Piaget, who was born in 1896 in Neuchâtel, Switzerland, and died in 1980. His theories have been expanded by other educators but stand as the foundation of today's classroom.

Piaget's Stages of Cognitive Development

Piaget is best known for his stages of cognitive development. He discovered that children think and reason differently at different periods in their lives, and he believed that everyone passes through a sequence of four distinct stages in exactly the same order, but the times in which children pass through them can vary by years. Piaget also described two processes that people use from infancy through adulthood to adapt: assimilation and accommodation. *Assimilation* is the process of using the environment to place information in a category of things you know. *Accommodation* is the process of using the environment to add a new category of things you know. Both tools are implemented throughout life and can be used together to understand a new piece of information.

Okay, did you assimilate and accommodate that? The main thing Piaget tells us is that kids really can't learn certain information and skills until they reach a certain place in their growth that is determined by years and behaviors. Understanding Piaget's stages is like getting the key to Learning City because it is a behavior map that tells you what your kids are ready to learn. Let's define the stages, then look at the behaviors. Piaget's four stages of cognitive development are:

1. *Sensorimotor stage (0 to 4 years):* In this period, intelligence is demonstrated through activity without the use of symbols (letters and numbers). Knowledge of the world is limited because it is based on actual experiences or physical interactions. Physical development (mobility) allows children to cultivate new intellectual abilities. Children will start to recognize some letters and numbers toward the end of this stage.

2. *Preoperational stage (4 to 7 years):* Intelligence is demonstrated through the use of oral language as well as letters and numbers. Memory is strengthened and imagination is developed. Children don't yet think logically very often, and it is hard for them to reverse their thinking on their own. Your little angel is still pretty egocentric at this age, and that is normal.

3. *Concrete operational stage (7 to 11 years):* As children enter this stage, they begin to think logically and will start to reverse

thinking on their own—for example, they will begin to complete inverse math operations (checking addition with subtraction, etc.). Expressing themselves by writing becomes easier. Logical thinking and expression is almost always about a concrete object, not an idea. Finally, children begin to think about other people more—they realize that things happen that affect others either more or less than they affect themselves.

4. *Formal operational stage (11 years and up):* As children become formally operational, they are able to do all of the things in the concrete operational stage—but this time with ideas. Children are ready to understand concepts and to study scientific theories instead of scientific discoveries. They can learn algebra and other math concepts not represented by concrete objects that can be counted. Whereas every stage until now has continuously moved forward, this is the only stage where a step back occurs. As a teenager, your child will become egocentric once again. It won't be easy for you. Thinking and acting as if the world exists exclusively for him or her is cute behavior for a five-year-old; it is rarely cute for a teenager.

Unfortunately, only 35 percent of high school graduates in industrialized countries obtain formal operations; many people will not ever think formally. However, most children can be taught formal operations.

The graph on page 16 puts the stages in a clear perspective.

Developmental Goals for Nine-Year-Olds

Now that you know the basics of developmental indicators, let's get down to the nitty-gritty of what can be expected from your fourth grader. A nine-year-old:

- Is industrious and impatient
- Is more coordinated than an eight-year-old

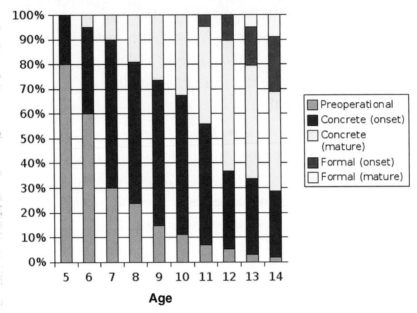

Percentage of Students in Piagetian Stages

Legend:
- Preoperational
- Concrete (onset)
- Concrete (mature)
- Formal (onset)
- Formal (mature)

Age

- Pushes himself or herself to physical limits
- Fatigues easily and is prone to injury
- Can be aloof
- Creates exclusive friendship groups
- Prefers the same gender
- Is competitive
- Wants to choose work partners
- Criticizes self and others
- Can become easily discouraged
- Sees adult inconsistencies and imperfections
- Complains about fairness issues

- Loves vocabulary and language play (but baby talk may reemerge)
- States things as negatives: "I hate it," "I can't," "boring," "yeah, right"
- Is still a concrete learner, but increasingly able to deal with multiple variables

Your nine-year-old is trying very hard to master the skills that he or she has been introduced to. This means working very hard at handwriting, arts and crafts, computers, drawing and/or any other skills that interest him or her. If the accomplishments don't come easily, there is a tendency to exaggerate feelings of inferiority. Redirection is the best solution here; criticizing your nine-year-old will have an effect that you will regret for years. This means that schoolwork and supplemental activities are better if short and to the point. Accomplishments should be displayed; cover every inch of your refrigerator with your child's latest and greatest. Nine-year-olds benefit from seeing their accomplishments on graphs or charts so that they can be reminded of successes while seeing the progression toward mastering a goal.

Developmental Goals for Ten-Year-Olds

Some fourth graders will turn ten during the school year. Here are some things you can expect from your ten-year-old. A ten-year-old:

- Switches from childlike behaviors to adultlike behaviors on a moment's notice
- Chooses extracurricular activities based on interest and abilities
- Claims to be "too old" for some activities or behaviors
- Is industrious and impatient
- Pushes himself or herself to physical limits
- Can be aloof

- Maintains important friendships outside of the classroom
- Becomes interested in the opposite sex
- Is competitive
- Wants to choose work partners
- Sees adult inconsistencies and imperfections
- States things as negatives: "I hate it," "I can't," "boring," "yeah, right"
- Embraces abstract thoughts

Now, you may be thinking, Oh no! My child is all over both lists! Remember, children vary greatly. It is common to find a two-and-a-half-year difference in development among children. Nine- to ten-year-olds who lag in specific skills often compensate by exceeding expectations in other areas of development. Don't worry. The best indicator of whether a child is in danger of falling behind is the rate of growth rather than an inventory of skills. If your child is making progress along the rough developmental continuum, don't be overly concerned about a few skills here and there.

Fourth Grade Learning 3

If you write it on the chalkboard, they will learn it. Sound familiar? If you are lucky, it doesn't—but for a great majority of people it is exactly how they were taught and were expected to learn. Luckily, in most schools, education has come to embrace children with different learning styles.

Learning Styles

Learning styles define how your child learns and processes information. Education experts have identified three main types of learning: visual, auditory, and physical. When learning a new math concept, for example, a visual learner will grasp the material more quickly by reading about it in a book or watching his or her teacher solve a problem on the blackboard. An auditory learner will understand the concept if she can listen to the teacher explain it and then answer questions. A physical learner (also known as tactile-kinesthetic) may need to use blocks, an abacus, or other counting materials (also known as manipulatives) to practice the new concept.

If you understand that your child is a visual learner most of the time—that is, he is most comfortable using sight to explore the world—you can play to his strength and incorporate physical and auditory learning styles when appropriate. It isn't unusual to interchange learning styles for different subjects. An auditory learner can easily use kinesthetic strategies to comprehend new math concepts.

Studies have shown that accommodating a child's learning style can significantly increase his performance at school. In 1992, the U.S. Department of Education found that teaching to a child's learning style was one of the few strategies that improved the scores of special education students on national tests. Identifying your child's learning styles and helping him within that context may be the single most significant factor in his academic achievement. Each activity in the subject area chapters of this book lists variations that help you tailor the activity to your child's learning style. Look for the symbols by the name of each learning style and use these styles to tailor the activities to your child's needs.

Learning styles are pretty easy to spot. All you have to do is watch your child's behavior when given a new piece of information.

👁 Visual

Would you give your right arm to get your child to listen to you? Are your walls a mural comprising every crayon your child has held? If you answered yes, you have a visual learner. You may not be able to get your child to follow two-step oral directions, but she can probably comprehend complex instructions when they are written on the blackboard or listed. Diagrams and graphs are a breeze. Your child can retell complex stories just by looking at one or two pictures from a book. Why is your child seemingly brilliant on paper but a space case when listening? Visual learners rely primarily on their sense of sight to take in information, understand it, and remember it. As long as they can see it, they can comprehend it.

Technically there are two kinds of visual learners: picture learners and print learners. Most children are a mixture of both, although some are one or the other (Willis and Hodson, 1999). Picture learners think in images; if you ask them what sound "oy" makes, they will likely think of a picture of a boy or a toy to remember the sounds of the letters. These kids like to draw—but you knew that by looking at your walls, right? Print learners think in language symbols: letters, numbers, and words. They would think of the actual letters "oy" to remember the sound they make together. Print learners learn to read quickly and are good spellers right off the bat. They also like to write.

Auditory

Is your child a talker? Is total silence the kiss of death to her concentration? Auditory learners understand new ideas and concepts best when they hear and talk about the information. If you observe a group of kids, auditory learners are the ones who learn a tune in a snap just from hearing someone sing it, or who can follow directions to the letter after being told only once or twice what to do. Some auditory learners concentrate better on a task when they have music or noise in the background, or retain new information more accurately when they talk it out. If you ask auditory learners what sound "oy" makes, they will recall the sound first and as many words as possible with that sound almost automatically.

Kinesthetic

Does your child need to touch everything? Physical learners (also known as tactual-kinesthetic learners—*tactual* for touch, *kinesthetic* for movement) use their hands or bodies to absorb new information. In some ways, everyone is a physical learner. If you peek into a classroom, you will see the physical learner tapping a pencil, a finger, or a foot, or twirling her hair to help her concentrate. These kids can't sit still and they are in the top percentile for being diagnosed with attention deficit disorder (ADD).

Before you run to the doctor because your child can't sit still, carefully observe him over a long period of time. Is the movement productive? Does he absorb or block information when moving? If he prefers to feel things in his hands or performs steady movement when trying to concentrate, he is engaging in productive learning.

Physical learners enjoy hands-on activities, such as cutting construction paper, sorting objects with their hands, and building elaborate projects. When you ask physical learners what sound "oy" makes, they will think of the physical cues used by the teacher or the cues they used when learning, such as tapping, physically picking the letters out of the alphabet, or holding *o* and *y* blocks.

Cognitive Learning

Cognitive learning levels are another way that teachers describe how a child processes information. I hear you asking, "Wow, how much of this do I have to remember?"—and you know I am going to say all of it, but it is really important. Let's recap for a minute to see how all of this fits together.

First, you learned about developmental stages, the physical growth that needs to happen before your child can learn certain things. Second, you learned about learning styles, the way your child prefers to process information. Third, you are about to learn about cognitive learning levels, the levels at which your child knows, understands, and can use information that he or she learns. Piaget identified the developmental stages in the 1930s and 1940s. By the 1950s, a group of researchers got together, led by Benjamin Bloom, and created the cognitive learning taxonomy designed to help you understand the levels of learning that can occur with new information. Bloom is often considered one of the most important educational theorists of the twentieth century. He was a professor at the University of Chicago who was more than a brilliant teacher: he was a brilliant thinker. Bloom spent his career researching how thinking and learning happened in students of all ages. Bloom and his researchers broke down the learning levels as follows:

Level 1: Knowledge. The things you know—bits of information that you can memorize, such as the ABCs.

Level 2: Comprehension. The things you understand—knowing the ABCs and understanding that they represent sounds.

Level 3: Application. The things you can apply—knowing the ABCs, understanding that they represent sounds, and then sounding out a word.

Level 4: Analysis. The things you understand well enough to think about them in a new way—knowing the ABCs, understanding that they represent sounds, sounding out a word, and then figuring out what the word means.

Level 5: Synthesis. Understanding something well enough to apply it to a new situation—knowing the ABCs, understanding that they represent sounds, sounding out a word, figuring out what the word means, and using it in a new way.

Level 6: Evaluation. Understanding something so well that you can tell if it is being used correctly—knowing the ABCs, understanding that they represent sounds, sounding out a word, figuring out what the word means, using it in a new way, and then figuring out if the new way is right.

Check the Bloom's Cognitive Learning Levels table on page 24 for some specific key words and behaviors for each level. Getting to know the key words will help you determine how to ask your child questions in order to find out the level at which your child understands new information. Use the examples in the right-hand column of the table to ask questions that check for each level of understanding.

Bloom's Cognitive Learning Levels

Cognitive Level	Verb	Key Words		Examples
Knowledge Recalls data. Exhibits memory of previously learned material by recalling facts and basic concepts.	Remember	choose define describe find how identify knows label list match name omit outline recall	recognize reproduce select show spell state tell what when where which who why	• Defines terminology/vocabulary • Describes details and elements • Recognizes classifications and categories • Knows principles, generalizations, theories, models, and structures • Knows subject-specific skills, algorithms, techniques, and methods • Names criteria for using certain procedures • Spells words • Outlines facts, events, stories, or ideas
Comprehension Demonstrates understanding of facts and ideas by organizing, comparing, translating, interpreting, giving descriptions, and stating main ideas. Understands the meaning, translation, interpolation, and interpretation of instructions and problems.	Understand	classify compare comprehend contrast convert defend demonstrate distinguish estimate explain extend illustrate	infer interpret outline paraphrase predict relate rephrase rewrite show summarize translate	• Summarizes or retells information • Translates an equation • Outlines the main ideas • Summarizes instructions, facts, details, or other things • Compares and contrasts ideas • Explains what is happening • Identifies statements to support a conclusion • Classifies information

Bloom's Cognitive Learning Levels

Cognitive Level	Verb	Key Words		Examples
Application Solves problems in new situations by applying acquired knowledge, facts, techniques, and rules in a different way. Uses a concept in a new situation or unprompted use of an abstraction. Applies what was learned in the classroom into novel situations.	Apply	apply build change choose compute construct demonstrate develop discover identify interview manipulate	model modify operate plan predict prepare produce relate select show solve utilize	• Applies a formula to solve a problem • Uses a manual to solve a problem • Describes how to use something • Finds examples to help apply ideas, rules, steps, or an order • Describes a result • Modifies ideas, rules, steps, or an order for use in another way • Selects facts to demonstrate something
Analysis Examines and breaks information into parts by identifying motives or causes. Makes inferences and finds evidence to support generalizations. Separates material or concepts into component parts so that its organizational structure may be understood. Distinguishes between facts and inferences.	Analyze	analyze assume categorize classify compare conclusion contrast discover dissect distinction distinguish	divide examine function inference inspect list motive relationships take part in test for theme	• Troubleshoots a problem using logical deduction • Lists components or parts of a whole • Names the function of something • Makes a distinction between two or more things • Classifies or categorizes a number of things • Draws a conclusion • Lists the parts of a whole

(continued)

Bloom's Cognitive Learning Levels *(continued)*

Cognitive Level	Verb	Key Words		Examples
Synthesis Compiles information in a different way by combining elements in a new pattern or proposing alternative solutions. Builds a structure or pattern from diverse elements. Puts parts together to form a whole, with emphasis on creating a new meaning or structure.	Create	adapt arrange build categorize change choose combine compile compose construct create delete design develop devise discuss elaborate estimate explain formulate generate happen imagine improve	invent make up maximize minimize modify organize original originate plan predict propose rearrange reconstruct relate reorganize revise rewrite solution solve summarize suppose tell test write	• Integrates training from several sources to solve a problem • Formulates a theory • Invents a solution • Constructs a model • Compiles facts • Minimizes or maximizes an event or item • Designs a solution, model, or project • Adapts something to create another thing
Evaluation Presents and defends opinions by making judgments about information, validity of ideas, or quality of work based on a set of criteria.	Evaluate	agree appraise assess award choose compare conclude criteria	importance influence interpret judge justify mark measure opinion	• Selects the most effective solution • Explains a selection, conclusion, or recommendation • Prioritizes facts • Rates or ranks facts, characters (people), or events • Assesses the value or importance of something

Bloom's Cognitive Learning Levels

Cognitive Level	Verb	Key Words		Examples
Evaluation (continued)				
Makes judgments about the value of ideas or materials.		criticize decide deduct defend determine disprove dispute estimate evaluate explain	perceive prioritize prove rank rate recommend rule on select support value	• Justifies a selection, conclusion, or recommendation

Adapted from Benjamin S. Bloom, *Taxonomy of Educational Objectives: The Classification of Educational Goals, by a Committee of College and University Examiners* (New York: Longmans, Green, 1956).

The Standards 4

Standards-based education came into the national spotlight over a decade ago. Communities and school districts previously made their own curriculum choices. For example, in one school district civics was taught in eighth grade and in another district it was taught in ninth grade, resulting in uneven and low test scores, because children were not taught the same subjects in the same grades but were tested on the same subjects.

The idea behind the standards reform movement is straightforward: when states set clear standards defining what a child should know and be able to do in certain grades, teachers and learners are able to focus their efforts and highlight particular areas in which they need improvement. Ideally, the standards show teachers what they need to teach by allowing curricula and assessments that measure performance to be aligned with the standards.

As with all reform movements, there are people who disagree with the idea of creating common learning standards. They primarily point to tendencies to simply "teach the test" and complain that the standards limit content breadth and community input. The real gripe may lie in the fact that education has always been a local issue. It is easy to fear change when you fear community values may be lost by standardizing state curriculum. Others believe that standards even the playing field. Before you form your own opinion, let's take a look at standards-based education.

Standards-based education lists content and skills that children need to learn at each grade level. Success depends on combining content and performance standards with consistent curriculum and instruction as well as appropriate assessment and accountability. This is the point where teachers and learners start to feel anxious. Everything sounds very official, particularly the accountability part. What does this language mean and what happens if children don't meet learning standards requirements?

Relax—there are no learning standards police patrolling our neighborhood schools, libraries, and bookstores. There are simply baselines by which the state determines eligibility for a high school diploma.

Let's start by defining learning standards.

Types of Learning Standards

Learning standards are broad statements that describe what content a child should know and what skills a child should be able to do in different subject areas.

Content standards are a form of learning standards that describe the topics to be studied, not the skills to be performed.

Performance standards are a form of learning standards that describe the skills to be performed, not the content to be studied.

Public school teachers must ensure that their students are taught the required content and skills because they are accountable not only to the students but also to their state, their school district, and their community for every child's performance on test scores. Private schools are accountable to their constituency with respect to student performance but not to the public. In fact, school requirements as well as teacher licensure are not as strictly monitored for private schools. The academically strong private schools institute internal standards that meet or exceed state expectations for public schools, but there are private schools that feel other aspects of child development, such as religious development, take precedence over academics. If your child attends private school, you must research the school to make sure it meets your expectations both academically and socially.

The use of testing to monitor classroom instruction is central to the theory of standards-based reform. It assumes that educators and the public can agree on what should be taught, that a set of clear standards can be developed, which in turn drive curriculum and instruction, and that tests can measure how well students perform based on those standards. There are two main types of standardized testing that your child will encounter:

1. Tests to determine individual student eligibility for promotion and graduation, college admission, or special honors. This type of testing has a long history. Examples include high school exit exams and college entrance exams, such as the Scholastic Aptitude Test (SAT) and the Advanced Placement (AP) test.

2. Tests that measure and compare school, school district, statewide, and national performance for broad public accountability. Increasingly, policy makers at the federal, state, and local levels want to identify ways to measure student performance in order to see how well the public education system is doing its job. The goals of this accountability approach include providing information about the status of the educational system, motivating desired change, measuring program effectiveness, and creating systems for financially sanctioning schools and requiring educators to receive more training based on the performance of their students.

It makes sense for you to make sure the content and skills that you work on with your child match the content and skills that the state has identified for that grade level. Children will do better on the standardized tests when more learning standards match assessment, or test, requirements. Legislation is in place that requires states to align their learning expectations with their testing expectations. The disconnect came when federal requirements for learning standards preceded testing requirements. Many states took the opportunity to test for content and skills that seemed more important than the ones enumerated in the learning standards. States and schools are working under federal guidelines to make all of the content match in a few years.

Learning Standards Resources

Each state has created a document that describes what children are supposed to know and what they are supposed to be able to do at each grade level and in each subject area. You may wonder who writes the standards and why you should believe that these people know what is best. A lot of public school teachers have wondered the same thing.

You can rest assured that writing the state learning standards is a collaborative effort. Most states rely on input from experts who know about the grade level and subject area. These experts could include teachers, researchers, people from the education industry, and school administrators. As an endnote or a footnote, each document lists the people hired by the state to help write the final version.

You can locate the standards that apply to your child through your state Department of Education's Internet site, by calling your state Department of Education, or through the Internet at www .knowledgeessentials.com. There are several things you should read for:

1. *Content standards*: What topics will your child be studying?
2. *Performance standards*: What skills must your child develop by the end of the year?

3. *Resources*: What resources are designed to help teachers meet the learning standards? Can you access them?

4. *Correlation reports*: Does the state provide a listing of how the required textbooks and other materials meet their own learning standards? Your school district should also be able to provide you with this information.

As you read your state's learning standards document, you may notice that you don't always agree with what is listed for your child to be learning. Is there anything you can do?

If your child attends a public school, there is little you can do to protest the prescribed curricula, but you can certainly enhance the curricula through learning activities at home. If your child attends a private school, you may have greater influence over classroom activities (as a paying customer), but you will probably not get the curricula changed to meet your concerns.

If you teach your child at home, then you have as much control as you would like over your child's curricula. You undoubtedly have specific beliefs that have led you to decide to homeschool, and you can remain true to those beliefs while still covering the required curricula. Even if you don't believe the required curricula are entirely appropriate, the assessments required by the states and higher education institutions will be normed to the learning standards of the state in which you live. The standards are just the basics that your child will need to succeed in mainstream society. There are many more opportunities for learning across a wide range of subjects that can be totally up to you.

Fourth Grade Reading 5

Fourth grade reading is about getting faster and better at reading. Your child already has the basic reading skills that are needed to be a good reader and will focus on using them with greater ease throughout the year. Children in the fourth grade will continue to work on the mechanics of reading, especially vocabulary skills, and expanding the number of words that they comfortably use. They will also be working quite a bit on reading comprehension, learning and using strategies to understand, interpret, and evaluate text. Do these skills look familiar? They should; your child is working on many of the same concepts that were learned in third grade but with a higher level of reading material.

Beginning of Fourth Grade Reading Checklist

Students who are working at the standard level at the beginning of fourth grade:

_____ Read with understanding and fluency

_____ Understand the meaning of synonyms, antonyms, and homonyms

_____ Identify the meanings of most compound words

_____ Use punctuation cues to add meaning to the text

_____ Use graphic organizers to aid comprehension

_____ Make reasonable predictions about something they are reading

_____ Identify the main idea of a passage

_____ Identify traits of characters in passages they are reading

_____ Summarize what has been read

_____ Know a large number of words by sight (don't have to sound them out)

Selecting Reading Material

To help your child with reading, it is important to help him select appropriate reading materials. There are various reading levels within a grade level. Have your child read a page out of a book; if he doesn't miss any words on the page, it is too easy. If he misses more than five words, it is probably too hard. Missing three to five words on a page usually means that the book is on the right level. There are usually codes on books to tell you the reading level and type of book. Check out www.knowledgeessentials.com to see a list of these codes.

It is also a good idea to have your child read a variety of genres of books. Some genres to choose from include realistic fiction, historical fiction, nonfiction, fantasy, poetry, science fiction, fairy tales, myths, and fables.

Your fourth grader might also want to read magazines and newspapers. Encourage her to do so. She will also learn about current events in your community, your state, and the world. This type of reading will most likely lead to some great conversations within the family. Being able to choose a magazine also lets children pick out a topic that interests them, because most magazines focus on a particular topic, such as sports or crafts.

The Mechanics of Reading

Reading skills for fourth grade students will focus on the following concepts: quotations and vocabulary. Let's cover the basic concepts for each, then move on to practical tips and activities.

Quotations

Reading dialogue and understanding how quotation marks are used can be confusing. Your child has been reading for a few years now and has seen quotation marks, so they are not completely foreign, but now he will be asked to understand all of the rules for using quotation marks correctly. Once your child knows the "hard rules" about quotation marks, he will be able to gain more understanding from reading text that uses them. What are some of these "hard rules"?

- We use quotation marks to show exactly what is being spoken.

- The quotation marks go around the spoken words.

- Each quotation begins with a capital letter.

- A comma separates the quote from the rest of the sentence, for example, Mom said, "I'm going to the store today."

- When a quote is an exclamatory or an interrogative sentence, the end punctuation goes inside the quotation marks. The following example is an interrogative (question) sentence. "When will we go to the beach?" I asked Mom.

- When we change speakers, we start a new paragraph.

Vocabulary

As your child gets older, her range of vocabulary also needs to increase. Most standardized tests have a section devoted to vocabulary. The larger the vocabulary base your child has, the more she will be able to comprehend. Knowing the meanings of multiple-meaning words and how the words are used in context will continue to be a part of the reading process. These words include synonyms, antonyms, and homonyms. Your child will also be learning how to use a thesaurus and a dictionary to help with learning vocabulary words.

The table on page 38 describes some of the important skills related to the mechanics of reading, where children can run into problems, and what you can do to help them along.

Mechanics of Reading Skills	Having Problems?	Quick Tips
Recognizes dialogue.	Has difficulty recognizing the words of a speaker.	Teach your child the trick of seeing the quotation marks as clothespins that hold up the words as something special for all to see and hear. (This also works with the titles of smaller works such as poems, articles, or songs. They're lighter than larger works, so they can hang. But books are heavier and have to sit on a shelf, so they are underlined.)
Uses dialogue.	Has difficulty punctuating dialog when the speaker is included in the sentence.	Again, make sure the words to be quoted are treated as something special to hang in the air, with proper punctuation included, and *then* include the speaker to begin or end the sentence.
Expands his vocabulary.	Has difficulty generating synonyms to enrich his own writing.	Keep synonym practice to adjectives and adverbs, which are good describing words. At dinner, ask for words describing, say, the broccoli—as many as possible. Help your child train his brain to think of new ways to express an idea. It will translate into his writing.

Mechanics of Reading Activities

 **Hunting Dialogue**

Learning happens when: your child looks through a newspaper or magazine article and hunts for dialogue inside quotation marks. He should highlight all of the sentences that have quotation marks around them. When your child has highlighted as many as he can, have him cut out the quotations and glue them onto construction paper. Read each quote together, and ask your child what the quotations have in common with one another. List the things he tells you on a piece of paper. He should be able to come up with some of the basic punctuation rules of reading and writing dialogue using quotation marks that were discussed at the beginning of this section.

Variations: You can also choose a fiction book. Instead of highlighting and cutting out the quotations, your child would need to copy the quotations or type them on the computer.

🖐 Kinesthetic learners should react well to the activity as written, since they get to do a lot of moving and manipulating objects during learning.

👁 Visual learners will learn by seeing the quotations all together on a page.

👂 Have your auditory learner read each quotation aloud and tell you the rules he comes up with.

Mastery occurs when: your child can identify the basic rules of using quotation marks.

You might want to help your child a little more if: he can't see the similarities in the quotations that he has selected. You might have to do a little coaching and point out two sentences that have something in common, then ask him about only those two sentences. Find two other sentences, repeat the procedure, and expand from there.

TIME: 20 minutes

MATERIALS
newspaper or magazine
highlighter
rounded-edge scissors
nontoxic glue
large sheet of construction paper
paper
pencils

2 Writing Dialogue

TIME: 30 minutes

MATERIALS
- paper
- pencils
- colored pencils

Learning happens when: you have your child write a conversation between herself and another person. When she has finished writing the conversation, have her go back and read her part while you read the other part. Make sure all of the rules have been followed, such as that a new paragraph should start when the speaker changes. Ask questions to lead your child to the things that need correcting. Finally, rewrite the whole conversation in colored pencils so that it is easy to see that the rules were followed. For example, your child's exact words can be written in blue. The other person's exact words can be written in red. Make the quotation marks and other punctuation marks green. The parts of the sentences that say who is speaking can be written in orange.

Variations: This activity could be done on the computer. Change the font color for each part by highlighting the text you want changed, going to the format tab and selecting the item for font, then selecting the color you want the text to be.

- Kinesthetic learners would probably prefer to do the activity on the computer because there are more things to manipulate.

- Visual learners will appreciate using the colors to create a visual aid.

- Auditory learners will get the most out of the activity as you both read the parts aloud. It would also be good to go back over each color the text is printed in and discuss why it is written in that way.

Mastery occurs when: your child can easily color code the dialogue correctly and explain the rules that go along with it.

You might want to help your child a little more if: she doesn't understand the rules of dialogue. Try writing the rules in colors and then helping your child write each part of the dialogue in the color of the rule. For example, with a red pencil write the rule about using quotation marks, and then write all quotation marks on the page in red. Using a blue pencil, write the rule for commas, and then make all commas on the page blue.

3 | Using a Thesaurus

Prepare a two-column chart on the paper. One column has a list of words, and the other column is for your child to write at least five synonyms for each word in the first column. See page 42 for an example. You want your child to use the words in a sentence, which he can say to you or write on a separate sheet of paper.

Learning happens when: you give your child the chart and ask him to think of five synonyms for each word. When he has come up with the synonyms, have him use each one in a sentence.

Variations: Try this activity with antonyms.

🖐 Kinesthetic learners could also act out the meaning of each word.

👁 Visual learners could draw a picture to illustrate each word.

👂 Auditory learners should read each word from the list, say the synonyms as they write them, and say the sentences aloud.

Mastery occurs when: your child can find synonyms for each word in the word list and use the synonyms correctly in a sentence.

You might want to help your child a little more if: he can't find a synonym for each word and/or use the synonyms in sentences.

TIME: 20–30 minutes

MATERIALS
▪ paper
▪ pencils
▪ list of words that have at least five synonyms (see the table on page 42 for one example. You can find other examples at www .knowledgeessentials.com)
▪ thesaurus

Try saying a word in a sentence to your child and then asking him to replace that word with one that means the same thing in the same sentence.

Word List	Synonyms
Empty	1.
	2.
	3.
	4.
	5.
Fast	1.
	2.
	3.
	4.
	5.
Said	1.
	2.
	3.
	4.
	5.
Great	1.
	2.
	3.
	4.
	5.
Angry	1.
	2.
	3.
	4.
	5.

Word List	Synonyms
Sick	1. 2. 3. 4. 5.
Old	1. 2. 3. 4. 5.
Hot	1. 2. 3. 4. 5.
Strong	1. 2. 3. 4. 5.

4 Homonym Charades

Write a word and its definition on the same side of a card. Make sure you have included the homonym and its definition on another card. For example, cards for both "deer" and "dear" should be included in the game. Label each card "Homonym Charades" on the back for future use.

TIME: 30 minutes

MATERIALS

index cards

list of homonyms with definitions (if you need a list of homonyms, you can find one at www .knowledgeessentials.com.)

crayons or markers

dry erase board

dry erase markers

dictionary

2–4 players

Learning happens when: you place the cards with the side labeled "Homonym Charades" up in the center of the players. Players take turns drawing a card. The player who draws the card acts out the meaning of the word while the others try to guess what the word is. Remember, the player acting out the word can't talk. Whoever guesses the word writes the correct spelling on the dry erase board. Then it is his or her turn to draw a card and act it out.

Variations: Try this activity with other parts of speech or word types. You can write words on the cards and then change the rules, such as act out a synonym of the word you draw or act out an antonym of the word you draw.

Kinesthetic learners love this activity because they get to move around and write the word on the dry erase board.

Have visual learners help you prepare the cards. They might even want to draw a picture on each card that illustrates the meaning of the word.

Auditory learners will learn best by saying the word and hearing others make guesses. It would be a good idea to have them spell the word aloud when they are writing it on the dry erase board.

Mastery occurs when: your child successfully associates the correct definition and spelling to each word.

You may want to help your child a little more if: she is having trouble identifying the correct word and its spelling. Start with fewer cards, but be sure to include the homonym of cards you do choose. When your child demonstrates mastery of those cards, add some more until she has mastered all of the cards.

5 Word Hunt

TIME: 20 minutes

MATERIALS
newspaper
highlighter
dictionary
notebook
pencils
crayons or markers

Learning happens when: your child reads the newspaper and highlights at least ten words he doesn't know the meaning of. Have your child write one word on a page of a notebook, look up the definition of the word in a dictionary, and write it down in the notebook. Then have your child write a sentence using the word, draw an illustration of the word, and color the illustration. Continue with the rest of the words.

Variation: This could become a daily activity in which your child finds a new word each day. You might also have him cut out the article in which he found the word and glue it onto the notebook page.

 Kinesthetic learners will enjoy highlighting and cutting out the articles and making the notebook.

 Visual learners will benefit from creating a visual dictionary of the words found.

 Auditory learners should review the words and their definitions aloud as they finish each page. It would also be a good idea to review the words every day.

Mastery occurs when: your child learns the meaning of the new words and can use them correctly in a sentence.

You might want to help your child a little more if: he can't use the new words correctly in a sentence. Try modeling a sentence for your child first. You may need to start a sentence for him to finish.

6 Definition Race

TIME: 30 minutes

MATERIALS

- list of vocabulary words (you can use a list from school or you can find a list at www .knowledgeessentials.com)
- index cards
- dictionary
- crayons or markers
- 2–4 players

Write words from the vocabulary list on some of the index cards. Write the definitions of the words on another group of cards. You may want to play this activity outside where you have plenty of room. Make sure it is not a windy day, or you will spend more time chasing the cards than identifying the words.

Learning happens when: you place the cards with the words only at one end of the yard. Make sure the cards are spread out and have the words facing up so you can see them. Stand at the other end of the yard with the definition cards and the players. Read one definition aloud. The players should run to the other end of the yard and find the word that goes with the definition. The player who finds the word card should run back and check the word and its meaning with you.

Variations: If you would rather do this activity indoors, you could put the words at the end of a hallway or attach them with Velcro to a piece of poster board. (You can buy poster board and small circular self-sticking pieces of Velcro at any discount store.)

- This activity is very appealing to kinesthetic learners because they get to run back and forth.
- It may help visual learners to have the definition written down for them to read themselves.
- Have auditory learners say the words aloud when they find them.

Mastery occurs when: your child can match the vocabulary words to the correct definitions.

You may want to help your child a little more if: she is having trouble matching the vocabulary words to the correct definitions. Try reducing the number of choices.

7 | Word for the Day

TIME: About 20 minutes over the course of one day

Learning happens when: your child writes the date down on one page in the notebook. Then he writes a word and its definition on the same page. If the word has more than one definition, your child should write down all of the definitions on the notebook page. The challenge is to use the word correctly five times in one day. Each time your child uses the word, he should write down the sentence in the notebook. At the end of the day, review with your child the ways he used the word.

MATERIALS
- vocabulary word of your child's choice
- notebook
- pencils

Variations: Ask your child to focus on one meaning of the word.

- Your kinesthetic learner could act out the meanings of the word.

- Visual learners will do well with this activity because writing down the word will give them a visual reminder.

- Auditory learners will do well with this activity because they are saying the word aloud throughout the day.

Mastery occurs when: your child can use the word correctly five times in one day.

You may want to help your child a little more if: he can't use the word correctly five times in one day. If it is a word with multiple meanings, limit the meanings to one or two.

8 | Question It

TIME: 20–30 minutes

MATERIALS
■ list of vocabulary words
(you can use a list
from school
or find a list at www
.knowledgeessentials.com)
■ dictionary
■ index cards
■ pencils

Learning happens when: your child writes one vocabulary word and its definition on one side of each index card. Shuffle the cards and then draw one card at a time. Have your child ask you yes or no questions about the word on the card such as "Is it an adjective?" "Is the word a place?" "Does the word describe an event?" When your child thinks she knows what the word is, she can make a guess.

Variations: You could also give clues about the word to help your child guess the word.

- 👐 Kinesthetic learners could act out their guesses.

- 👁 Visual learners could write down your answers to their questions.

- 👂 Auditory learners will do fine with the activity as it is written because most of the activity is done orally.

Mastery occurs when: your child is able to guess most of the vocabulary words.

You might want to help your child a little more if: she is having trouble identifying the vocabulary words. Try limiting the number of words you work with each time. Make sure you always include some words you have worked with before for review.

9 | ABC Vocabulary

Learning happens when: your child chooses a topic and then brainstorms a list of vocabulary words that go with the topic. There should be one word for each letter of the alphabet. For example, for the topic of sports your child might choose the words "archery," "baseball," "cross-country skiing," "downhill skiing," "equestrian," "football," "golf," "hockey," "ice skating," and so on. Next, have your child fold eight sheets of paper in half to form a book. Staple the pages together at the fold. Your child should write one vocabulary word and its definition on each page of the book, then draw and color an illustration for each word.

Time: 20–30 minutes

Materials
- paper
- stapler
- pencils
- colored pencils

Variations: Include a sentence for each vocabulary word. Make the sentences tell a story throughout the entire book.

Kinesthetic learners might want to cut out their own illustrations or illustrations from a magazine and glue them into the book.

This activity is good for visual learners because they are drawing an illustration to go with each vocabulary word.

Auditory learners should read each word and its definition aloud as they are creating the book and then reread it when the book is completed.

Mastery occurs when: your child can recall the definitions of the words in his book.

You might want to help your child a little more if: he is having trouble remembering the definitions of the words. Try focusing only on parts of the alphabet at one time. For example a–g, then h–m, o–s, and finally t–z.

Comprehension

What fun is it to learn new words if you don't understand how to use them? Reading comprehension gives your child the opportunity to practice using words in context. Seeing a word in context brings a whole new level of understanding of the word and the nuances of its meaning.

The typical fourth grade student will be reading from a wide variety of books. Most of these will be longer-chapter books, so it is a good idea to discuss with your child what he has been reading every day. Your child will continue to identify the parts of a story as well as other strategies that will help him to comprehend, interpret, and evaluate the text.

Comprehension Skills	Having Problems?	Quick Tips
Can retell what he just read.	Leaves out important parts of the story.	It helps to read what your child reads. That way you can actively ask questions to help him fill in important gaps. "Wait, who did that?" "Now, where did that happen?" "Are you sure that happened first?"
Can retell what she just read.	Includes too much unimportant detail.	Be sure to aid your child in staying focused. Again, ask questions, but this time make sure you're not rushing your child; you're just helping her get back to the point of the story.
Can relate personally to what he is reading.	Does not understand the significance of an event.	Do your best to help your child recall a time in life when he might have experienced a feeling or situation similar to that in the reading. Then help him see the connection.
Can visualize what's happening in her reading.	Misses details due to a lack of visualization.	Reread to your child after she has read on her own. Stop occasionally to have your child add to a picture in her mind. It should be a picture that grows more detailed as more information is added. The visualization allows for faster, easier comprehension; your child will need to do less rereading as she trains her brain to "see" the story as it happens.

The table on page 50 describes some of the important skills related to reading comprehension, where children can run into problems, and what you can do to help them along.

Comprehension Activities

1 Visualize It

Learning happens when: your child reads a chapter of a book and visualizes the description of a character, the setting, or an event in his mind. Then he should take a piece of paper and draw the image he pictured. Make sure your child also colors the picture; this helps to bring out the details in the story. Finally, he should share the description with you.

Variations: Your child could do the drawing on the computer with a paint program or with clip art. You could also read a passage to him and have him illustrate the scene for you.

- Kinesthetic learners could make a three-dimensional model of their visualization.
- Visual learners will work well with the activity as written since they are creating a visual representation.
- Auditory learners will get the most out of orally describing the visualizations to you.

Mastery occurs when: your child can draw a picture that accurately represents something from the book.

You might want to help your child a little more if: he can't accurately draw an illustration of something in the book. Try rereading a short passage to your child and then having him illustrate the passage.

TIME: 30 minutes

MATERIALS

- interesting book (see appendix A for suggestions)
- paper
- pencils
- colored pencils

2 Fluency Building

TIME: 15–20 minutes daily

MATERIALS
- paper
- pens or pencils
- familiar book (or passage from a book)
- stopwatch

Create a chart like the one below on a piece of paper, or print a copy from www.knowledgeessentials.com.

Name of Book	Date	Number of Words Read	Number of Mistakes

Learning happens when: you and your child choose a familiar story that you both enjoy. Use the stopwatch to time your child as she reads aloud for one minute. As your child reads, mark any mistakes she makes on a piece of paper. Stop your child after one minute and record the date, the number of words read, and the number of mistakes on the chart. Show your child the mistakes she made during the reading.

Each night, have your child read the same passage. As she reads, the number of words read in one minute should increase, while the number of mistakes should decrease. Continue with this passage until your child can read it fluently without mistakes. Change the passage as she increases her reading level.

Variations: There are not too many ways to do this activity. You can choose from a variety of types of reading material, however, such as newspapers, poetry, or magazines.

Kinesthetic learners might tap or move their feet while reading. Sometimes any kind of movement helps kinesthetic learners to focus.

Visual learners will be comfortable because the whole activity is visual.

This is also excellent for auditory learners because they are reading aloud for the activity.

Mastery occurs when: your child can read for one minute without making any mistakes.

You may want to help your child a little more if: she is not able to correct previous mistakes and increase the amount of words read in one minute. Find a passage that is at a lower reading level so your child will be able to succeed.

3 | Identifying Parts of a Story

Create a graphic organizer like the one on page 54 on a piece of paper or print one out from www.knowledgeessentials.com.

Learning happens when: you and your child discuss the information about the story listed on the graphic organizer and fill in the answers.

Variations: You might choose to have your child do the activity on his own rather than with you. Before you begin, you might want to brainstorm a list of the events that happened in the story. Then your child can evaluate or choose which events were the most important. Once he has made a choice, he will need to put the events in the correct sequence.

TIME: 20–30 minutes

MATERIALS
- pencils
- paper
- recently read story (the first time you do this activity, choose a short, interesting story you have read together)

Title of book	
Setting	
Main characters Name and a short description	
Main conflict	
Main events in sequence	
Resolution How was the conflict solved?	

✍ Have kinesthetic learners write the events from the story on individual cards so that they can manipulate them and put them in the correct sequence.

👁 Your visual learner might want to also have a space on the graphic organizer to draw and color a small picture to go with the information.

👂 Auditory learners might want to present the information to you in a news report. Your child could report it into a tape recorder.

Mastery occurs when: your child can identify all the parts of a story he has read.

You might want to help your child a little more if: he is having trouble identifying some part of the story. See which parts he does not understand and then reread those parts with him. You can model how you would do it. Give him a chance to identify part of it with you guiding by asking questions related to that part.

4 | Character Chart

Create a chart like the one below on a piece of paper, or print one
out from www.knowledgeessentials.com.

Time: 20–30 minutes

Materials
- pencils
- paper
- recently read book

Name of Character	
Brief description of character	
Character's actions	1. 2. 3. 4.
Character traits	1. Example: 2. Example: 3. Example: 4. Example:
Character's feelings	1. Example: 2. Example:
Character's motives	1. Example: 2. Example:

Learning happens when: your child fills in the chart with information about a character from a book she has read.

Variations: Your child could use a cluster graph to organize the information. A cluster graph is made by drawing a circle around a main idea, such as "character traits" and then drawing other circles linked to that main idea with lines. In each of these circles is written something that relates to the main idea, such as "smart" or "funny."

Character: Charlotte

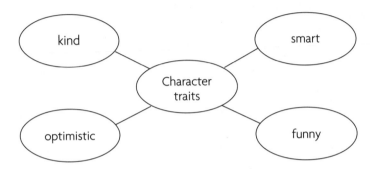

You can find other examples at www.knowledgeessentials.com.

- Kinesthetic learners could act out some of the scenes when they are describing the character's actions.

- Visual learners could have an extra column in the chart to illustrate one example for each item describing the character.

- Auditory learners could make a radio commercial describing the character to others.

Mastery occurs when: your child can fill in the chart with an accurate description of the character.

You might want to help your child a little more if: she can't fill in the chart with information about the character. You might try having her fill out the chart as she is reading the book instead of waiting until she has finished the entire book.

5 | Cause and Effect

Create a cause-and-effect chart like the one below or print one from www.knowledgeessentials.com.

TIME: 20–30 minutes

MATERIALS

pencils
paper
book

Cause	Effect
Didn't sleep all night	Fell asleep at school

Learning happens when: you give your child some examples of cause and effect. For example, you might say that you didn't sleep all night, and the next day you fell asleep at work. Ask your child what happened to you. He should reply that you fell asleep at work. Write that in the "Effect" column in the cause-and-effect chart. Ask him why you fell asleep or what caused you to fall asleep. Write the cause in the appropriate column. Continue to give examples and have your child find the cause and the effect. When he understands those concepts, read a short book. Have him identify some causes and effects from the story and write them down in the same chart.

Variations: Your child could give you some examples and have you choose the cause and the effect.

✋ Kinesthetic learners could act out the situations before choosing the cause and the effect.

👁 Visual learners could select some examples of cause and effect from pictures or television shows.

◐ Auditory learners will do fine with the activity as it is written because most of it is done orally.

Mastery occurs when: your child can accurately choose the cause and the effect from a situation.

You might want to help your child a little more if: he can't choose the correct cause and effect. Help by asking your child appropriate questions to guide him to the correct answer.

6 Venn Diagram

TIME: 20–30 minutes

MATERIALS
▪ paper
▪ pencils
▪ book

A Venn diagram is made up of two or more overlapping circles. It is often used in mathematics to show relationships between sets. For our purposes here, it will be used to show the traits that two storybook characters have in common. Create a Venn diagram like the one below (or print one out from www .knowledgeessentials.com).

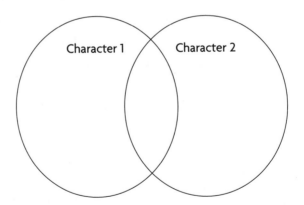

In each circle, your child should write things that describe what is unique to each character. In the section where the two circles intersect, she should write down the things the two characters have in common.

Learning happens when: your child reads the book and picks out two of the characters to compare and contrast.

Variations: Your child could also compare herself to another family member using a Venn diagram. There are any number of things you can compare using this tool.

- 🖐 Kinesthetic learners could make a physical Venn diagram out of rope and put actual items in the circles, such as foods, hobbies, or favorite items.

- 👁 Visual learners could add a small visual aid beside the words in each circle of the diagram.

- 👂 Auditory learners could use the Venn diagram to give an oral report comparing and contrasting the two characters.

Mastery occurs when: your child can fill out the Venn diagram to compare and contrast two characters.

You might want to help your child a little more if: she can't fill out the Venn diagram to compare and contrast the two characters. Try using a favorite bedtime story to compare and contrast two familiar characters.

7 | News Article Details

Copy the chart on page 60 on a piece of paper, or print one out from www.knowledgeessentials.com.

Learning happens when: you have your child read the newspaper article and then fill out the chart with details of the event described in the article. Then have your child write a short summary of the main ideas and details of the article in complete sentences.

TIME: 20–30 minutes

MATERIALS
- newspaper article
- paper
- pencils

Title of Article	
Who is the article about?	
What is the article about?	
Where did the event take place?	
When did the event take place?	
Why did the event take place?	

Variations: You could use this form for your child to write a summary of each chapter as he reads a book.

✋ If your child is a kinesthetic learner, you could have him use a highlighter while reading the article to highlight the parts that answer the questions.

👁 Your visual learner might want to draw small pictures to go with each question.

👂 Have your auditory learner say the answers aloud to you after you ask the questions. Have your child read the summary back to you.

Mastery occurs when: your child can accurately answer the questions about the newspaper article and then rewrite the main ideas and details of the article.

You might want to help your child a little more if: he can't answer the questions about the article. You can help your child use a highlighter to mark the information that will answer the questions.

8 What's Next?

Learning happens when: your child chooses an activity and creates steps to teach someone how to do it. This will help your child with sequencing and giving directions. First, have your child brainstorm some activities that she could write directions for. Some examples might be how to blow a bubble or how to make a peanut butter and jelly sandwich. When your child has chosen an activity, she will need to brainstorm the steps needed to accomplish the task. Then she will need to put the steps in order and write them down.

Variations: Your child could gather the supplies needed for her activity, then hand out the written directions and demonstrate the procedures for the audience.

TIME: 20–30 minutes

MATERIALS
- paper
- pencils

Kinesthetic learners would do best with this activity by doing the procedure physically and writing the directions as they finish each step.

Visual learners might also want to include a small illustration with their directions.

Auditory learners will benefit from saying the steps aloud and might also want to record the directions on tape.

Mastery occurs when: your child can write a set of directions to complete a task.

You might want to help your child a little more if: she can't write the directions in sequential order. Help her to perform the procedure and write the directions as she completes each step.

9 Comic Strip

TIME: 20–30 minutes

MATERIALS
- recently read book
- paper
- colored pencils

Learning happens when: your child picks eight events from the book he has recently read. He should put the events in sequential order. Have your child divide the piece of paper into eight rectangles—one for each event from the book. Then have him illustrate and write dialogue or a sentence for each event in one of the rectangles to make a comic strip. When all of the rectangles are completed, have your child color the illustrations.

Variations: You could have your child use poster board to make a larger comic strip.

✋ Kinesthetic learners should do fine with the activity as written because they will be moving the paper around and illustrating each square. If your child does have trouble focusing, try allowing him to act out each square before he draws it.

👁 Visual learners will especially enjoy the activity as written because it is so visual.

👂 Auditory learners could read or record the dialogue for the comic strip.

Mastery occurs when: your child can choose the main events in a story and retell them to someone else in the proper sequence using words and pictures.

You might want to help your child a little more if: he can't find enough events in the story or puts the events in the wrong order. You may have to guide him by asking questions.

Environmental Learning

Once children have the tools to read words, the best way you can help them become lifelong readers is to expose them to a variety of activities and people. Life experiences are a big part of reading. For example, children who play soccer will be able to fully understand the parts of a story that features a soccer game or a soccer player. Trips to museums, plays, sporting events, musical events, and the zoo all provide a learning experience for children that can enhance their reading comprehension and breadth of vocabulary.

End of Fourth Grade Reading Checklist

Students who are working at the standard level at the end of fourth grade:

_____ Read with understanding and fluency

_____ Use graphic organizers to aid comprehension

_____ Visualize descriptions and details

_____ Can follow and give sequential directions

_____ Can summarize a story

_____ Can use past experiences to identify with a character

_____ Compare and contrast various things

_____ Understand cause-and-effect relationships

_____ Can use basic rules with quotation marks in dialogue

Fourth Grade Writing 6

In fourth grade, your child will probably be asked to write in cursive all or at least much of the time. Writing becomes even more important in all of the subjects, even math. Your child will be expressing his or her thoughts and ideas, as well as what has been learned, in book reports, research papers, essays, and poetry. Fourth graders continue to review and practice the parts of speech as well as learn how to make them plural and possessive. Your child will be writing to inform others, persuade others, and to express himself or herself in many ways.

Beginning of Fourth Grade Writing Checklist

Students who are working at the standard level at the beginning of fourth grade:

_____ Communicate in writing

_____ Use writing to inform others

_____ Use writing to persuade others

_____ Can identify nouns, verbs, adjectives, and adverbs in a sentence

_____ Use adjectives to describe things and enhance their writing

_____ Use conjunctions

_____ Use common spelling rules

_____ Identify sentence types

_____ Write compound sentences

Grammar and Writing

Your child is at the age where grammar skills are going to be getting more complicated, so let's review them to avoid any confusion as you go along.

Basic Grammar Concepts

Helping your child grapple with grammar can get confusing, so let's take a look at two grammar concepts that you should be prepared to help your child with, now and for the next ten years: the basic parts of speech and sentence fundamentals.

The Basic Parts of Speech

adjective   A word that modifies a noun; it describes a quality of a person, place, or thing.

adverb   A word that describes a verb, an adjective, or another adverb; it often ends in *ly*.

conjunction   "Junction what's your function? Hookin' up words and phrases and clauses." As the classic *Schoolhouse Rock* song tells us, conjunctions are words such as "and," "or," and "but" that connect words, ideas, phrases, clauses, and sentences into one big sentence or idea.

interjection   An exclamation or utterance such as "wow," "oh," or "huh."

noun   Names a person, place, thing, feeling, idea, or act.

plural noun   Refers to two or more people, places, or things.

proper noun   Names a particular person (someone's name), place, or thing and begins with a capital letter.

preposition   Shows the relationship between one noun and a different noun, verb, or adverb, such as "in" or "through."

pronoun   Replaces a noun, such as "he," "they," or "it."

singular noun   Refers to one person, place, or thing.

verb   Describes action.

verb tense   Tells you when the action happened. The main forms are present (I sing), past (I sang), future (I will sing), present participle (I am singing), and past participle (I have sung).

Sentence Fundamentals

What makes a sentence? For a group of words to be a sentence it needs three things:

1. The words make sense and express a complete thought.

2. It begins with a capital letter and ends with a period, exclamation point, or question mark.

3. It contains a predicate and a subject. The predicate, or verb, tells what the subject, or noun, is doing.

Sentences can be any length, as long as they follow these rules.

The parts of a sentence include:

direct object   A noun or pronoun that is having an action done to it.

indirect object   A noun or pronoun that tells you for what or whom the action of the verb (predicate) is being done.

predicate   The verb that describes what the noun (subject) of the sentence is doing or being.

subject   A noun or pronoun that is performing the verb; the "doer" of a sentence.

The following are examples of subject and predicate:

1. Brittany runs the mile.

   Brittany is the subject; *runs the mile* is the predicate; *runs* is the verb; *mile* is the direct object.

2. Matt's brother threw Luke the football.

   Matt's brother is the subject; *brother* is the simple subject; *Matt's* is an adjective (possessive, proper adjective); *threw Luke the football* is the predicate; *threw* is the verb; *Luke* is the indirect object; *football* is the direct object.

A **compound sentence** is two sentences joined together using a conjunction. The most common conjunctions are "and," "although," "as," "because," "but," "if," "or," "though," "where," and "whether." Conjunctions that indicate time are: "before," "after," "until," "since," "when," "whenever," and "while."

The following sentences show how conjunctions are used:

Amy sold the blue coat *and* it was dirty.

Amy sold the blue coat *because* it was dirty.

Amy sold the blue coat *before* it was dirty.

Notice how the conjunctions change the meaning of the sentence, so choosing the right one is important!

(continued)

Types of Sentences

declarative   A sentence that makes a statement. A declarative sentence ends with a period.

Example: Marcus is a basketball player.

imperative   A sentence that is a command. An imperative sentence ends in a period. The subject of an imperative sentence is always understood to be you, even though "you" is not stated in the sentence.

Examples: Shut the door. Go to bed. Wash the dishes.

exclamatory   A sentence that expresses strong feelings or emotions. An exclamatory sentence ends in an exclamation point.

Examples: We won the game! Ow, that hurt!

interrogative   A sentence that asks a question. An interrogative sentence ends in a question mark.

Examples: Do you want to go to the park? What are we having for dinner?

The Writing Process

Your child will be writing a lot this year and for years to come. Writing just doesn't happen; there is a process. Let's call it the writing process. It consists of these six main steps:

1. Brainstorming—writing down as many topics or ideas you can think of in a short amount of time.

2. Prewriting—organizing your ideas; this can include making a cluster graph (see page 79) or outlining your information.

3. Drafting—writing your first copy. Make sure your child knows he or she will write the paper more than once. This always seems to surprise students.

4. Revising—on your own or with a partner. The partner should compliment the writer and give suggestions on what to add or maybe remove from the writing.

5. Editing—also known as proofreading. You and/or a partner should read your copy, looking for misspelled words, incorrect capitalization, and punctuation.

6. The final copy.

Helpful samples and organizers for the writing process are available at www.knowledgeessentials.com.

Grammar and Writing Skills	Having Problems?	Quick Tips
Can identify the parts of a sentence.	Has difficulty differentiating between the parts of a sentence (namely the subject and the predicate).	Create or find a few sentences with your child. Draw a vertical line between the "who or what" of the sentence and the "action" of the sentence. This will show that any simple sentence has only two parts. Once that's done, more details of the specific parts of speech can be addressed.
Can recognize and create various types of sentences.	Has difficulty differentiating between the types of sentences.	Keep a list of the types of sentences and their descriptions handy. Pull sentences from magazines or make up your own. Help your child master one type at a time by recognizing end punctuation and/or the message of the sentence. Togetherness is the key. As soon as your child can teach you, he has mastered the concept.
Can use the writing process.	Has difficulty following the steps or chooses to skip steps.	Help your child relate writing to any task in that there are specific steps to follow in sequence. For example, when making a pizza you can't put the toppings on before the sauce. The finished product is always better when all the steps are done in order. Graphic organizers also help, such as having your child fill in blanks and bubbles.

The table on page 69 describes some important skills related to grammar and writing, where children can run into problems, and what you can do to help them along.

Grammar and Writing Activities

1 Replace with a Pronoun

TIME: 30 minutes

MATERIALS
- list of pronouns (you can find one at www .knowledgeessentials.com)
- list of simple sentences
- dry erase board
- dry erase markers
- eraser for dry erase board

Learning happens when: your child writes one of the sentences on the dry erase board and reads the sentence aloud. Ask him to identify the nouns in the sentence. When your child can identify the nouns, ask him to look at the list of pronouns and find one that can replace the nouns. Your child should then rewrite the sentence with the pronouns instead of the nouns on the dry erase board and read the new sentence aloud. Ask him if the sentence still makes sense. For example:

A1. Marcus and Hillary went to the store.

A2. They went there.

B1. Andrew went to the mall to buy a shirt.

B2. He went there to buy it.

Variations: You don't have to use a dry erase board. You could have your child use paper and pencil, chalk and a chalkboard, or a word processing program on the computer.

✍ The kinesthetic child will learn best from this activity by using either the dry erase board or the chalk board.

👁 Visual learners might want to illustrate the sentences, writing the pronoun next to the picture it represents.

👂 Auditory learners will benefit from reading the sentences aloud.

Mastery occurs when: your child can replace the nouns with pronouns in the sentences and the sentences still make sense.

You might want to help your child a little more if: he is unable to replace the nouns with pronouns and still have the sentences make sense. Try limiting your sentences to those that use only specific pronouns. When your child has mastered those, move on to another group of pronouns.

2 Pronoun Shakeup

Learning happens when: your child cuts the index cards into squares large enough to write one pronoun on each square. Make enough squares to write each of the pronouns on its own square. Have your child write the pronouns and put all of the pronoun squares in the paper bag and shake it up. Have her draw one pronoun square out of the bag. She should read the pronoun aloud, then make up a sentence using the pronoun, and write it down. Continue with this procedure until there aren't any more pronoun squares in the bag.

TIME: 15–20 minutes

MATERIALS
- index cards
- crayons or markers
- list of pronouns (you can find one at www .knowledgeessentials.com)
- paper bag

Variations: You could have your child draw out two pronouns at a time and use them both in a sentence. If you do it this way, you might want to have each pronoun on more than one square in the bag. If your child draws two of the same pronoun, then she will need to draw another pronoun square to replace the duplicate.

✍ Kinesthetic learners will enjoy the activity as it is because they get a chance to be in motion.

👁 You might want to have your visual learner write all of the words in the sentence in black except for the pronouns, which she can write in red.

👂 Have your auditory learner read each sentence aloud as well as the pronouns.

Mastery occurs when: your child can use pronouns in a sentence so that the sentence makes sense.

You might want to help your child a little more if: she can't use pronouns in a sentence correctly. Try limiting the number of pronouns at first. When your child is successful with those, add more pronouns to the bag.

3 Adjective Shakeup

TIME: 15–20 minutes

MATERIALS
- index cards
- crayons or markers
- list of 20–25 adjectives (you can find one at www.knowledge essentials.com)
- paper bag

Learning happens when: your child cuts the index cards into squares large enough to write one adjective on each square. Make enough squares for at least twenty to twenty-five adjectives. Have him write one adjective on each square and put all of the adjective squares in the paper bag and shake it up. Have your child draw one adjective square out of the bag. He should read the adjective aloud and then make up a sentence using the adjective and write it down. Continue with this procedure until there aren't any more adjective squares in the bag.

Variations: You could have your child pull out two or three adjectives at a time and use them in a sentence.

👋 Kinesthetic learners will enjoy the activity as it is because they get a chance to be in motion.

👁 You might want to have your visual learner write all of the words in the sentence in black except for the adjectives, which he can write in red. You could also have your child illustrate the noun that he used the adjectives to describe.

Have your auditory learner read each sentence aloud as well as the adjectives.

Mastery occurs when: your child can use adjectives in a sentence so that the sentence makes sense.

You might want to help your child a little more if: he can't use adjectives in a sentence correctly. Try limiting the number of adjectives at first. When your child is successful with those, add more adjectives to the bag. Also ask such questions as "what kind?" "how many?" or "what did it look like?" to help him choose an adjective to use.

4 | Singular to Plural

Learning happens when: you go over the following rules with your child on changing a singular noun to a plural noun.

Singular	Plural
Most singular nouns	add s Example: doll—dolls
Nouns that end in ch, sh, s, or sh	add es Example: beach—beaches
Nouns ending with a vowel and a y	add s Example: birthday—birthdays
Nouns ending with a consonant and a y	change the y to i and add es Example: party—parties

Next, your child should cut the index cards into squares just large enough to write one singular noun. Have your child write one of the singular nouns on each square, and then put the squares into the paper bag.

TIME: 20 minutes

MATERIALS
- index cards
- list of 20 or 25 singular nouns (You can find a list of singular nouns appropriate for this activity at www .knowledgeessentials.com)
- list of the singular nouns made plural
- paper bag
- paper
- pencils

Then your child should pull a square out of the bag, read the word on it aloud, and write it on a piece of paper. She should then look at the rules again to decide what needs to be done to the word to make it plural, then write the plural noun down beside its singular version. Continue until all of the singular nouns have been changed into plural nouns.

Variations: After your child is successful with the activity, she could do it in reverse, starting with the plural form, then writing down the singular form. When the activity has been completed, your child could put the plural words into categories based on the rules for changing the nouns to the plural form.

- This activity will work well for kinesthetic learners the way it is because they are able to move around when they draw the squares from the bag.

- It will help visual learners to look at the chart of the rules for forming plurals. At the end of the activity, they should look back over the words they have written.

- Auditory learners should say each word in both the singular and plural forms. It would be a good idea to have them repeat the rules aloud as well.

Mastery occurs when: your child can change the singular words into the plural form based on the rules in the chart.

You might want to help your child a little more if: she is having trouble changing the singular nouns into plural nouns. Start by limiting the nouns to two categories: those that add s and those that add *es*.

5 It's Mine

Learning happens when: your child takes a singular noun and adds an apostrophe and an *s* to change the word into a singular possessive noun. Then your child should write a sentence with the singular possessive noun. An example would be the noun "dog." He should add an apostrophe and an s to make the word "dog's." Ask your child what belongs to the dog, and then have him write a complete sentence with the singular possessive noun. For example, The dog's bone was large and tasty. Have your child continue changing nouns into singular possessive nouns and writing sentences with them.

Variations: You could change the activity by telling your child the noun and what it owns, then having him come up with a sentence and writing it down. For example, tell your child the dog has a bone. Then he will need to make it into a singular possessive noun and use that in a sentence.

TIME: 15 minutes

MATERIALS
list of singular nouns
paper
pencils

✌ Have kinesthetic learners find an object somewhere in the house, then write a sentence using a singular possessive noun that goes with that object. For example, if he chooses a plate, the sentence might be: Mom's plate is very beautiful.

👁 Visual learners could write the rest of the sentence in one color and the singular possessive noun in a contrasting color to make it stand out.

👂 Auditory learners do best if they read the sentence aloud, emphasizing the singular possessive noun.

Mastery occurs when: your child can change a singular noun into a singular possessive noun and use it correctly in a sentence.

You might want to help your child a little more if: he is having problems changing the noun into a singular possessive noun or using it in a sentence. Hold up an object from your house and ask your child whom it belongs to. Help him to write it correctly in a sentence. Continue practicing this way until he can do it on his own.

6 Haiku

TIME: 30 minutes

MATERIALS
- paper
- pencils
- crayons or markers

Learning happens when: you explain to your child that a haiku is a kind of poem invented by the Japanese. It has three lines, and none of them have to rhyme. In a haiku the first line always contains five syllables, the second line always has seven syllables, and the last line always has five syllables. Haiku are often about nature. The following is an example:

The sea was stormy.
Seashells were left on the shore.
I gathered them up.

Have your child decide on a topic and then brainstorm things about the topic. Have her come up with the first line of a haiku about that topic using one of the ideas. Check to make sure it has only five syllables. Proceed with the next two lines, making sure they each have the appropriate amount of syllables. Each line should also be about the same subject.

Variations: Your child could rewrite the haiku on decorative paper or illustrate it.

✋ Kinesthetic learners do best with this activity if they clap out each line to check for the correct amount of syllables. Each syllable gets one clap.

👁 Visual learners should illustrate their poems.

⑨ Auditory learners should read each line aloud and clap to check for the correct amount of syllables. At the end of the activity, they should read the entire poem aloud.

Mastery occurs when: your child writes a poem with the correct amount of syllables on each line.

You might want to help your child a little more if: she is having trouble getting the correct amount of syllables for each line. Try helping to clap it out. Suggest words that could be added or deleted to help with the syllable count.

7 │ Diamonte Poem

Learning happens when: you go over the form of the diamonte poem with your child.

TIME: 30 minutes

MATERIALS
- paper
- pencils

The following is the diamonte form:

Line 1—one noun

Line 2—two adjectives that describe the noun in line 1

Line 3—three participles ending in ing that tell about the noun in line 1

Line 4—four nouns; the first two relate to the noun in line 1 and the last two relate to the noun in line 7

Line 5—three participles ending in ing that tell about the noun in line 7

Line 6—two adjectives that describe the noun in line 7

Line 7—one noun

The nouns in lines 1 and 7 usually are opposites. The following is an example of a diamonte poem:

Ocean
wet, large
swimming, floating, surfing
waves, fish, cactus, snake
sweating, sunning, searing
hot, dry
Desert

Have your child choose a subject and brainstorm a list of words that could go with the subject (noun). Next, he should choose another subject (noun) that is the opposite of the first one and brainstorm a list of words that would go with it. Go through the poem form line by line to help your child write the poem using the words he has chosen.

Variations: You could have your child write the poem on a particular theme. You could also have him type it on the computer with word processing software or create a presentation, with each line on one page, in PowerPoint.

✍ Kinesthetic learners would probably do best with this activity by typing it on the computer and adding clip art or his own computer graphics to enhance the poem.

👁 Visual learners learn best by illustrating the poem in some way.

👂 Read the directions line by line to auditory learners and have them read the finished poem aloud.

Mastery occurs when: your child can write the poem in the correct form.

You might want to help your child a little more if: he can't write the poem with the parts of speech in the correct form for the poem. Try giving hints of a word that would work, or suggest one word and have your child come up with the other ones.

8 | My Best Friend

Learning happens when: your child uses the writing process to write an essay about her best friend. The first step is for your child to decide on a best friend. Once that has been decided, it's time to brainstorm everything she can think of about that person. All of these things should be written down for later use; the brainstorming could be recorded as a list. The next step is to organize the information. This can be done in many ways. I like to use a web or cluster graph like the one that follows. (This and other helpful organizers are available at www.knowledgeessentials.com.)

TIME: Varying amounts of time

MATERIALS
- paper
- pencils

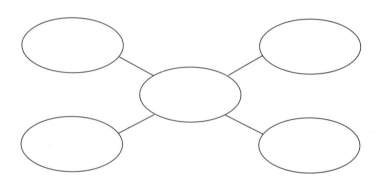

Variations: Try the same activity with more focus—ask your child to write about how her best friend plays ball or how her best friend earned her latest scout patch.

- Kinesthetic learners will like to imitate their friends by acting out a portion of what they write.

- Visual learners like to draw pictures that go with what they write. Suggest that your child find photos of her friend to go with what she writes instead of drawing this time.

- Auditory learners will enjoy orally expanding the stories that they write. Ask your child to tell you more about her friend.

Mastery occurs when: your child writes about her friend in an organized manner.

You may want to help your child a little more if: her essay about her friend isn't in a sequential or logical order or if the essay doesn't make sense. Try taking what your child wrote and together inserting the ideas into a web or a cluster graph. After you have reorganized the information that way, ask your child to write one section of the essay at a time, talking about what will be in each section before she writes.

Environmental Learning

Writing mechanics, grammar, and punctuation rules are a part of daily life. Have some fun with your kids as you drive down the street by pointing out mistakes made on signs such as when someone does not use an apostrophe correctly. When you find errors in the newspaper or in magazines, share them with your child. Encourage him to find mistakes. The better you and your child become at scoping out errors, the more likely it is that he won't make those mistakes. The best way to really learn the rules of writing is for him to become a rule enforcer.

Writing, like reading, is a cornerstone to learning for the rest of your child's life. Support development of your child's writing skills by reading what he is writing and then talking to him about the parts that are good and the parts that can be a little clearer. Adults naturally consider grammar and punctuation along with word choice when writing. Your child is just starting to learn how to do this. Your expertise and guidance will be invaluable as he learns to communicate clearly in writing.

End of Fourth Grade Writing Checklist

Students who are working at the standard level in fourth grade:

____ Use the writing process to compose

____ Use various sentence types appropriately

____ Use both simple and compound sentence structures

____ Understand the parts of a sentence

____ Use a broader vocabulary to express themselves

____ Write in cursive neatly and consistently

____ Recognize and use proper punctuation

Fourth Grade Math 7

Fourth grade math is a characterized by skill building and growth. Your child has learned many new mathematic concepts during the elementary years. Third grade, in particular, was a year of many new concepts. This year your child will be refining his or her abilities.

In third grade, your child learned to add and subtract larger numbers, both with and without regrouping. She learned basic multiplication and division facts, estimated sums and differences by rounding, learned to find geometric and number patterns, and learned to read and write numbers up to one million. Your child also began using fractions to describe parts of a whole and parts of a set, comparing fractions, and working with equivalent fractions. Last year she was asked to name, describe, and compare both shapes and solids, figure elapsed time, measure to the nearest inch, find both perimeter and area, and understand new concepts, such as congruency, symmetry,

---

Beginning of Fourth Grade Math Checklist

Students who are working at the standard level at the beginning of fourth grade:

_____ Comfortably add and subtract large numbers

_____ Know the basic multiplication and division facts

_____ Understand how place value works in our number system

_____ Can round numbers in order to make a reasonable estimate

_____ Use tools, such as rulers and thermometers, to measure

_____ Can differentiate solids from shapes

_____ Can find fractions of a whole and fractions of a set

_____ Understand basic probability and statistics

_____ Understand how bar graphs, line graphs, and tables communicate information

and coordinate graphing. Finally, your child was asked to tell whether events were more likely or less likely to occur, to find permutations of up to three items, and to collect, organize, and record information.

Fourth graders will build on those concepts learned in third grade. The concepts your fourth grader will learn this year can be divided into four broad categories:

- Operations and computation
- Number sense and patterns
- Geometry and measurement
- Data analysis and probability

Number Operations

Last year, your child learned to add and subtract three- and four-digit numbers, both with and without regrouping. This year, he will be reinforcing these skills through review practice. He may be asked to add or subtract numbers greater than four-digits, but it should not be difficult because the procedure is the same regardless of the size of the number. Your child also used rounding to estimate sums and differences, which is another skill that will be reinforced this year. In third grade, your child learned the basic multiplication and division facts. This year will begin with a quick review of those facts. If your child is rusty on the facts, help him learn them as soon as possible, because a big part of the fourth grade operations is multiplying larger numbers and long division. Your child will also be asked to apply various estimation strategies, including rounding, to simplify computations.

To help your child learn to multiply larger numbers, he will be taught about the associative property of multiplication. The associative property, or grouping property, of multiplication means that if you are multiplying three or more numbers, you can multiply them in any groups and get the same answer. This means that you can take a problem like

$6 \times 2 \times 3 =$ ____ and you can solve it by multiplying $(6 \times 2) \times 3 =$ ____ or $6 \times (2 \times 3) =$ ____ or $(6 \times 3) \times 2 =$ ____ and you will get the same answer. (It is important to make sure you are using an $\times$ as the multiplication sign; your child hasn't yet learned to use a $*$ as the multiplication sign.) Deciding how to group a problem to most easily solve it is one of the mental math strategies your child will learn this year. The following table describes some skills related to number operations, where children can run into problems, and what you can do to help them along.

Number Operations Skills	Having Problems?	Quick Tips
Estimates the product of two- and three-digit numbers to solve problems.	Does not understand the purpose of estimation.	Explain that the purpose of estimation is to find an approximate answer instead of an exact answer. Also, estimation should be easier to do mentally than the actual computation.
Rounds numbers to the nearest tens place.	Has trouble rounding.	The most common way of estimating is rounding the numbers before multiplying. Make sure your child knows how to round. Start by rounding a two-digit number to the nearest ten. Use a number line, if necessary, to see to which ten the number is closest. This should be simple, except if there is a five in the ones place. The five is right in the middle between two tens. If there is a five in the ones place, it automatically is rounded up. Once your child is comfortable rounding a two-digit number, round a three-digit number to the nearest hundred. Again, ask to which hundred is the number closest? Your child should be able to answer. If the tens place has a five, the number will automatically round up to the next hundred.

(continued)

Number Operations Skills	Having Problems?	Quick Tips
Can find the product of two- and three-digit numbers.	Confuses which numbers to multiply.	Be very intentional on what type of problems to do first. Have your child multiply two-digit numbers by one-digit numbers first (e.g., 42 × 5). Make sure he remembers to regroup. Once he is comfortable, move on to a three-digit number times a one-digit number (e.g., 312 × 6). Then move on to a two-digit number times a two-digit number (e.g., 65 × 21); a three-digit number times a two-digit number (e.g., 718 × 52); and finally, a three-digit number times a three-digit number (e.g., 903 × 482).
Puts a place saver in problems.	Forgets to put a place saver (zero) in the problem.	Forgetting the zero is a common but very detrimental mistake. The place saver is vital, and forgetting it will result in an incorrect answer. Practice with your child, reminding her about the place saver, until she remembers to use it.
Lines up numbers properly.	Has trouble keeping numbers lined up properly.	This is another common problem. Multiplication demands neatness. If your child has trouble lining up the numbers properly, he will have trouble adding to find the final answer. A simple solution is to use graph paper. The rule is that only one digit can be put in each box. This solution has helped many fourth graders keep things straight.

Number Operations Skills	Having Problems?	Quick Tips
Can estimate the quotient of the problem with a one-digit divisor and a two- or three-digit dividend (e.g., 39 ÷ 8).	Has trouble estimating in division.	Estimating in division is a little different from estimating in multiplication. To estimate in division, find a dividend that is a multiple of the divisor. For example, in 39 ÷ 8, the multiples of 8 are 8, 16, 24, 32, 40, 48, etc. The multiple closest to 39 (our dividend) is 40. So, mentally divide 40 by 8. The answer is 5. So, 39 ÷ 8 estimates to about 5. A three-digit number works on the same principle. For example, in the problem 419 ÷ 6, look at 419. Four (the number in the hundreds place) is less than 6 (our divisor), so look at the hundreds and tens place (41). The multiples of 6 include 6, 12, 18, 24, 30, 36, 42, etc. The multiple 42 is closest to 41 (in 419), so 41 is replaced by 42, and the 9 becomes a zero. Our new problem is 420 ÷ 6, which is 70. This is fairly complicated, but once your child understands the steps and practices, it will become easier.
Can find the quotient of a problem with a one-digit divisor and a 2- or 3-digit dividend.	Has trouble with long division.	First, make sure your child knows the basic multiplication and division facts. If the facts are known, your child is most likely confusing the steps. The steps to long division are divide, multiply, subtract, and bring down. A mnemonic device to remember the steps is "Dogs Might Start Barking." Dogs = divide, Might = multiply, Start = subtract, Barking = bring down. Work with your child until she has the confidence to complete a problem on her own.

(continued)

Number Operations Skills	Having Problems?	Quick Tips
Uses a variety of estimation and mental math techniques to simplify and solve computations.	Has trouble computing mentally.	Many children have trouble figuring a problem in their heads. The solution is just to practice. Have a quick quiz. Ask your child to do one math problem in her head sometime during the day. Start with simpler problems and build on them.

Number Operations Activities

1 Triangular Flash Cards

TIME: 15–20 minutes

MATERIALS

- index cards
- rounded-edge scissors
- crayons or markers (2 different colors)

Learning happens when: you have your child help you make the flash cards. Bend one corner of each index card until it reaches the opposite side of the card and make a fold. It should look like a triangle on top of a rectangle. Cut off the rectangular piece at the bottom, which will leave you with a square, which has been folded to look like a triangle. Open up the triangle and cut along the fold line to create two triangles. Once you have several triangles, turn them so that the longest side is on the bottom, with the point pointing up. On the bottom corners of one triangle, write two numbers to be multiplied, using one color of marker. On the top corner, write the answer, using a second color of marker. It takes some time to make these, but they are worth the work. Hold the flash cards so that your thumb is covering the top corner and have your child multiply the bottom numbers. Remove your thumb to reveal the answer. Your child can also do this on his own, and the flash cards provide immediate feedback on whether the answer was right or wrong.

Variations: Hold the flashcards so that one of the bottom corners is covered. Your child now has flashcards for the division facts.

The top number is the dividend, and the bottom number showing is the divisor. The answer is covered by your thumb.

✋ Kinesthetic learners will enjoy making the flash cards. Once they understand how the flash cards work, let them hold the flashcards.

👁 Visual learners will like to help you make the flash cards.

👂 If your child learns by listening, have him say the entire fact, instead of just the answer.

Mastery occurs when: your child can quickly say the facts and knows how multiplication and division are related.

You may want to help your child a little more if: he is feeling frustrated over all the facts. Start with a smaller number of facts. Have your child experience more successes by learning a few facts very well before adding more facts to the flash cards.

2 | Multiplication War

Remove the face cards from the deck and make the aces equal to one.

Learning happens when: you and your child play the card game War with a new set of rules. To play, deal the entire deck of cards between the two of you. You and your child will each flip over two cards at the same time to create two two-digit numbers. One of you will multiply the two numbers on paper, while the other checks on the calculator. If the person working on paper gets the correct answer, she wins all four cards. If the answer is incorrect, the person with the calculator gets the four cards. Then switch so that the person on the calculator is now figuring on paper, and the

TIME: 10–15 minutes

MATERIALS
- deck of cards
- paper
- pencils
- calculator

person figuring on paper now has the calculator. Continue to switch roles after each round. The winner is the person with the largest number of cards after all of the cards have been played.

Variations: Both of you do the calculations on paper. The person who figures first wins the cards. If there is a disagreement on the answer, use the calculator to check.

✍ Kinesthetic learners will enjoy taking turns figuring and then checking with the calculator.

👁 Visual learners may want to line the cards up to resemble a multiplication problem.

👂 Auditory learners may need to think aloud as they figure the solution.

Mastery occurs when: your child successfully multiplies the numbers together.

You may want to help your child a little more if: she is having trouble multiplying the numbers. Practice more with your child before competing.

③ Estimation Races

TIME: 15 minutes

MATERIALS
▪ index cards
▪ crayons or markers

On a piece of paper, write several multiplication problems, as in the first column of the table on page 91.

Write one estimated answer obtained by rounding, as shown in the third column of the table, on each index card.

Learning happens when: you spread out the index cards at one end of the room and designate a starting point on the other side of the room. Call out one of the multiplication problems. Your

Original Problem	Estimated Problem Using Rounding	Estimated Answer
24 × 11	20 × 10	200
36 × 23	40 × 20	800
16 × 58	20 × 60	1,200
53 × 35	50 × 40	2,000
41 × 64	40 × 60	2,400
78 × 45	80 × 50	4,000
94 × 67	90 × 70	6,300
73 × 96	70 × 100	7,000
356 × 249	400 × 200	80,000
112 × 592	100 × 600	60,000
677 × 449	700 × 400	280,000
806 × 951	800 × 1,000	800,000
737 × 192	700 × 200	140,000

child's task is to estimate and solve the problem by rounding to the nearest ten, hundred, or thousand. When your child has an answer, he should race to the opposite end of the room, retrieve the answer, and bring it back to you. Call out a second math problem and have your child estimate the answer by rounding and find the estimated answer across the room. Continue until you have gone through all of the problems.

Variations: This game can be used for any of the operations: addition, subtraction, multiplication, or division. Children who love competition could compete directly against another person, perhaps an older brother or sister.

✋ This activity will appeal to your mover and shaker.

👁 Have visual learners help write the index cards.

👂 If your child learns best by listening, have him verbalize the steps to estimate the answer as he is computing.

Mastery occurs when: your child can easily estimate multiplication problems by rounding.

You may want to help your child a little more if: he is having trouble finding the correct answer. Make sure your child can accurately round the numbers. Then have him show you the estimate in order to get the green light from you to race across the room.

4 | Domino Division

TIME: Varying amounts of time

MATERIALS
- dominoes
- 8 index cards
- paper
- pencils

Learning happens when: your child plays a division game using dominoes. Turn the dominoes upside down and mix them up. Write the digits 2 through 8 on the cards, one digit per card. Shuffle the cards and place them facedown in a pile. You and your child each pick one domino. There are two parts on each domino. One part will be the tens place, and the other part will be the ones place. Turn the domino to make the largest number possible. For example, this is the same domino turned two ways.

This way, the number is 52.   This way, the number is 25.

Because you want to create the largest number, turn the domino to make the number 52. This number is the dividend.

After you and your child both have your numbers, have her flip over one of the index cards. This number is the divisor. For example, if your child flips over a 6, the division problem is 52 ÷ 6. Your problem will be different, unless you picked the same domino that your child did. Next, you both will figure your division problem. The person who figures correctly and has the largest quotient collects the two dominoes. If you both have the same quotient, look at the remainder to determine a winner. The larger remainder wins. Return the index card to the pile and shuffle the cards. When you have gone through all of the dominoes, the person with the most dominoes wins.

Variations: For those kids who get pumped up when competing and take pride in being fast, try this variation: Flip only one domino and one index card. The person who comes up with the correct answer first wins the domino.

- ✋ Kinesthetic learners will enjoy using the cards and dominoes to make division problems.

- 👁 Have your visual learner try working the problem on a small dry erase board.

- 👂 Your auditory learner may need to verbalize the steps as she performs them.

Mastery happens when: your child correctly solves the division problems.

You may want to help your child a little more if: she is having problems dividing. Use the dominoes to create practice problems instead of as a tool for competing. When your child has practiced enough to feel comfortable figuring the quotients, add the competitive element.

5 | Capture Ten

TIME: 15–20 minutes

MATERIALS
- 10 small pieces of paper, numbered 1 through 10
- 3 dice
- paper
- pencils

Learning happens when: you and your child use math operations to capture as many numbers as possible. Lay out the ten pieces of paper, numbered one through ten. The first player rolls the three dice. Using only the three numbers rolled, the player uses addition, subtraction, multiplication, and/or division to capture as many of the paper numbers as possible. For example, 3, 1, and 4 are rolled. You can capture one ($4 - 3 \times 1 = 1$), two ($4 - 3 + 1 = 2$), six ($4 + 3 - 1 = 6$), seven ($4 + 3 \times 1 = 7$), eight ($3 + 1 + 4 = 8$), and so on. After the turn, the ten pieces of paper are returned to the center of the table and are used by the second player. Use the paper and pencil to keep score by counting how many numbers are captured in each turn. After five rounds, the person who captured the most total numbers wins.

Variations: Work together to see how many numbers the two of you can catch. This variation appeals to those students who prefer to work together rather than compete.

✋ Kinesthetic learners will enjoy throwing the dice and capturing the pieces of paper.

👁 Visual learners may need to use pencil and paper to work out various solutions.

👂 Have your auditory learner verbalize what he is doing. It will also help if you verbally work out your problems as well as doing them on paper.

Mastery occurs when: your child can think of ways to use several different operations to capture several numbers.

You may want to help your child a little more if: he can only capture numbers by using only one operation. Work together and model how to use more than one operation to capture numbers.

6 │ Three in a Row

Make a hundreds chart by drawing a 10×10 grid and filling in the numbers 1 through 100, one number per box, or print one from www.knowledgeessentials.com.

Learning occurs when: you and your child play a game to capture three numbers in a row. The object of the game is to get three of your markers in a row somewhere on the hundreds chart. The row can be vertical, horizontal, or diagonal. You and your child will roll a die to see who goes first. The first player rolls all three dice and uses any operation on the numbers rolled to capture a number. This is very similar to the previous game, Capture Ten. The only difference is that a player can use two of the dice to create a two-digit number. For example, if the player rolls a 3, 1, or 4, many numbers can be created ($4 - 3 \times 1 = 1$; $4 - 3 + 1 = 2$; $4 - 1 + 3 = 6$; etc.) In addition, players can use the 3 and 1 to create the number 31 and add the 4 ($31 + 4 = 35$) or subtract the 4 ($31 - 4 = 27$). Players can create the number 13 and add the 4 ($13 + 4 = 17$) or subtract the 4 ($13 - 4 = 9$). There are many possibilities. However, each player can only use one of these problems to make one number per turn. She will put a marker on that number, which can now no longer be captured. Player two will then roll the dice, look at the possible captures, and then pick one number to capture. Play continues until someone has captured three in a row. After playing this game a few times, your child will probably become more sophisticated in her use of math and will use more difficult operations, such as division and multiplication.

Variations: If three in a row is too easy, try to capture four in a row. Or, you can make any number available for capture (even ones that have been captured before). Switching out game pieces will provide additional opportunities to capture three in a row as well

TIME: 20–30 minutes

MATERIALS
- paper
- pencils
- 3 dice
- 20 game pieces, 10 each of 2 colors or shapes, such as 2 different types of dried beans, 2 different colors of poker chips, or 2 different types of pasta

as additional opportunities to block your opponent from doing the same.

👋 Kinesthetic learners will enjoy this activity because there's plenty of movement.

👁 Visual learners are good at seeing where they should put their markers on the board.

👂 Auditory learners will benefit from verbalizing the problems they use to capture a number and from hearing you explain your thinking.

Mastery occurs when: your child can find many possible numbers to capture with each roll of the dice.

You may want to help your child a little more if: she is relying on very simple ways to capture a number. You may want to help her by saying, "Oh, I see you can also get a 13." If your child asks how, try to get her to figure it out on her own. If your child just cannot figure it out, give a small clue, such as multiply and then subtract. If she still cannot figure it out, let her capture another number and then show your child how the number could have been captured.

Number Sense and Patterns

In fourth grade, there will be an emphasis on finding the rule in number patterns and solving simple math sentences using a variable. Your child will start by putting a variable in the space where they write the answer, for example, $2 + 2 = y$. After your child is comfortable seeing a variable there, you can put the variable somewhere else, $2 + y = 4$, and then regroup (using the associative property) to get $4 - 2 = y$, and find the answer for y.

Place-value skills are being extended to larger numbers in fourth grade. Your child will apply place-value concepts on numbers through the millions. One of the best ways to get place-value concepts across to children is with money. They understand that there is a big difference between $1,000 and $100,000. In addition, they will explore decimals by reading, writing, renaming, comparing, and ordering decimals to the hundreds place. Again, you can use dollars and cents as a way to work with decimals at home.

Your child will also explore fractions, with an emphasis on understanding how fractions and decimals are related. You can turn a decimal into a fraction by putting the numbers on the right of the decimal point as the numerator and the place value of the number to the farthest right as the denominator. For example, the decimal .35 is the fraction $^{35}/_{100}$ because the 5 is in the hundreds place. Your child will also discover, describe, extend, and create a wide variety of patterns, using tables, graphs, rules, and models.

The following table describes some skills related to number sense and patterns, where children can run into problems, and what you can do to help them along.

Number Sense and Pattern Skills	Having Problems?	Quick Tips
Solves simple math problems using a variable.	Is confused by the variable.	Many students think of the equals sign in math as a cue to "find the answer." If the answer is already given, sometimes students get confused. Start with simple sentences, such as $3 + a = 5$. Explain that the letter is a secret number. Your child must find the secret number that goes in the math sentence. If he cannot see the answer right away, start testing different numbers to see if they work in the sentence. After doing a few, your child should start understanding what a variable is and how to solve for it.

(continued)

Number Sense and Pattern Skills	Having Problems?	Quick Tips
Uses place-value concepts up to the millions.	Is confused by place value.	Math is very predictable. Place value is also very predictable. Sometimes all the numbers and commas are confusing to students. Color-code place value in numbers (for example, blue for hundreds, red for tens, orange for ones). Also, explain that the commas stand for a word in the number. For instance, if the number has one comma in it, as in 2,412, the comma stands for the word "thousand." If the number has two commas, the first comma stands for the word "million," and the second comma stands for the word "thousand." All a student needs to understand is how to read a three-digit number (which most can by fourth grade) and what to say when she comes to a comma.
Can read, write, rename, compare, and order decimals to the hundreds place.	Does not understand decimals.	Make sure your child understands that decimals stand for part of a number, for example, that 2.5 is more than 2 but less than 3. If your child ate $2\frac{1}{2}$ pieces of pizza last night, he ate 2.5 pieces of pizza. Find examples of when decimals are used, such as body temperature, timed sporting events, and money. Discuss with your child what those decimal numbers mean.
Can read decimals.	Has trouble reading decimals.	Explain to your child that there are three parts to read in a decimal. The first is the number to the left of the decimal. That is the whole number. After reading the whole number, your child will come to the decimal. The decimal is read as the word "and." The last part is the number after the decimal. If there is one digit after the decimal, say the number and the word "tenths." So, 3.4 is read as "three and four tenths." If there are two digits after the decimal, read the two-digit number and say the word "hundredths." So, 13.53 is read as "thirteen and fifty-three hundredths."

Number Sense and Pattern Skills	Having Problems?	Quick Tips
Can understand the relationship between decimals and fractions.	Does not understand how decimals and fractions are related.	If your child learns to say a decimal properly as detailed previously, the relationship between the fraction and the decimal is stated. 3.4 is read as "three and four tenths," which is the same as $3\frac{4}{10}$. 13.53 is read as "thirteen and fifty-three hundredths," which is the same as $13\frac{53}{100}$.
Uses equivalent and nonequivalent fractions to compare, add, or subtract.	Has trouble comparing fractions.	The best way to compare fractions is to use fraction models. Ask your child's teacher if you can borrow a fraction model for a few days, or go to an education supply store. To compare $\frac{2}{3}$ and $\frac{3}{4}$, your child will compare the model of $\frac{2}{3}$ to the model of $\frac{3}{4}$ and see which is larger.
Can subtract fractions.	Has trouble adding and subtracting fractions.	Your child will most likely be adding fractions with like denominators. Many students mistakenly think that you add both the numerator and the denominator, so $\frac{1}{3} + \frac{1}{3}$ would equal $\frac{2}{6}$. To correct this, ask your child a series of 1 + 1 questions, using different items (for example, What is one cat plus one cat? What is one truck plus one truck?). After asking several questions, ask, What is one-third plus one-third? Using the same pattern as the series of questions your child just answered, she should say two-thirds.
Can discover, describe, extend, and create patterns.	Has trouble finding patterns.	You can very easily find items to make patterns, especially in the kitchen. Use colored candy, such as M&Ms or Skittles. Make patterns first with color. A pattern could be red-blue-red-blue-red-blue, red-red-green-red-red-green, etc. Have your child say the color pattern aloud (discover and describe). Then have him add the next two or three items to the pattern (extend). Finally, ask him to create a pattern for you to find and extend. Once your child can do color patterns, go on to number patterns.

(continued)

Number Sense and Pattern Skills	Having Problems?	Quick Tips
Can find the rule in number patterns.	Has difficulty finding the rule in number patterns.	Ask your child to notice first whether the numbers are going up or down. If the numbers are going up, the pattern will be either addition or multiplication. If the numbers are going down, the pattern will be either subtraction or division. Start with simple patterns. Have your child identify which operations the pattern can be. Once the options are narrowed down to two operations, look at the numbers to identify the operation being used.

Number Sense and Pattern Activities

1 Place Value Flip

TIME: 15–20 minutes

MATERIALS
- 2 index cards
- pencils
- deck of cards

Draw a large comma on each of the index cards. Prepare the deck of playing cards by removing the tens and the face cards. Make the aces represent the number one.

Learning happens when: you deal all the playing cards equally between you and your child. Have him flip over seven cards. He will make the largest number he can with the seven cards and the two comma cards. He should place down the following: one playing card, one of the comma cards, three playing cards, another comma card, and the last three playing cards. Have your child then read the seven-digit number. If he reads the number correctly, he scores one point. Your child scores another point if he made the largest possible number. When your child scores ten points, he is declared a place-value master.

Variations: After making the largest possible number, have your child rearrange the cards to make the smallest possible number.

Award one point for reading the new number correctly and another point for creating the smallest possible number.

✍ Being able to experiment with the digits by moving them around will help kinesthetic learners.

👁 Seeing how the digits can be moved around to create a number will help visual learners.

👂 Reading the number aloud will give auditory learners additional reinforcement.

Mastery occurs when: your child knows how to arrange the cards to create the largest possible number and can say the resulting number.

You may want to help your child a little more if: he does not understand how to create the largest number. Play the game with your child, taking turns. Watching you create the largest number and listening to you say it will serve as a model for him.

☐2☐ Which Is More?

Remove the tops of all the egg cartons so that only the bottoms remain. Leave one egg carton bottom whole. Your child can use this visual model of a whole bottom to better see the fractions of the whole. Take another bottom and cut it in half lengthwise so that there are two strips of six sections. Write "½" on each of the two strips. Take another egg carton bottom and cut it into thirds by making two vertical cuts, so that there are three pieces with four sections in each piece. Label each piece "⅓." Take another egg carton bottom and cut it into fourths by making a horizontal cut and a vertical cut. There should be four pieces, with three sections in each piece. Label each piece "¼." Take another egg carton and

TIME: 10–15 minutes

MATERIALS
- 6 egg cartons
- rounded-edge scissors
- permanent marker
- 22 index cards

cut it into sixths by cutting pieces with two sections in each piece. Label each piece "⅙." Take the last egg carton bottom and cut apart each section. You now have twelve pieces. Label each piece "¹⁄₁₂." On each index card, write one of the following fractions: ½, ⅓, ⅔, ¼, ²⁄₄, ¾, ⅙, ²⁄₆, ³⁄₆, ⁴⁄₆, ⁵⁄₆, ¹⁄₁₂, ²⁄₁₂, ³⁄₁₂, ⁴⁄₁₂, ⁵⁄₁₂, ⁶⁄₁₂, ⁷⁄₁₂, ⁸⁄₁₂, ⁹⁄₁₂, ¹⁰⁄₁₂, ¹¹⁄₁₂.

Learning happens when: you explain to your child that to make ⅔, you would take two of the ⅓ pieces. To make ⅚, you would take five of the ⅙ pieces, and so forth. Shuffle the index cards and place them facedown. Have your child draw two index cards. Use the egg carton fractions to create the models stated on the card. Have your child compare the two fractions and tell which fraction is larger. One point is awarded for each correct answer. When she reaches ten points, she is declared a fraction-comparison wizard.

Variations: Make this a game so that you each draw one card and create the fraction stated on the card. The person who drew the larger fraction is awarded a point. The first to reach ten points wins the game.

- Your kinesthetic learner will get a better sense of the fractions by creating the egg carton fractions herself, with guidance from you.
- Actually having the models of the fractions to compare will help your visual learner.
- Auditory learners will benefit from thinking aloud as they work.

Mastery occurs when: your child can successfully compare two fractions.

You may want to help your child a little more if: she is having trouble comparing fractions. First, make sure your child can create the fraction on the card with the egg carton pieces. If not, provide guidance until she understands. If she can create the fractions but has trouble comparing them, ask her to count the little sections. The fraction with the most sections is the largest.

3 | Which Are Equivalent?

On each paper plate, write one of the following fractions with one of the markers: ½, ⅓, and ¼. On the six index cards, use the other marker to write the following fractions: ²⁄₄, ²⁄₆, ³⁄₆, ³⁄₁₂, ⁴⁄₁₂, and ⁶⁄₁₂.

TIME: 10–15 minutes

MATERIALS
- 3 paper plates
- 6 index cards
- 2 crayons or markers of different colors
- egg carton fraction pieces (as detailed in the previous activity, "Which Is More?")

Learning happens when: your child uses the egg carton fraction pieces to find equivalent fractions. Shuffle the index cards and place them facedown. Draw an index card. Use the egg carton fraction pieces to create that fraction. Your child should then compare the fraction to ½, ⅓, and ¼ to see which one is its equivalent. Place the index card with the equivalent fraction on the paper plate. Have your child continue to draw cards, create fractions, and find equivalent fractions until all the cards have been used. At the end, your child should have ²⁄₄, ³⁄₆, and ⁶⁄₁₂ on the paper plate labeled ½; ²⁄₆ and ⁴⁄₁₂ on the ⅓ paper plate; and ³⁄₁₂ on the ¼ paper plate.

Variations: On the paper plates, write one of the following symbols: <, >, and =. Shuffle the index cards and place them facedown. Draw two cards, create the fractions, and put the appropriate paper plate between the two cards to show the relationship between the two fractions.

✋ Using the egg carton fraction pieces will help kinesthetic learners understand fractions better.

👁 Visual learners will benefit from seeing the relationships between the fractions.

👂 Auditory learners will benefit from discussing their observations with you.

Mastery occurs when: your child can find equivalent fractions.

You may want to help your child a little more if: he is having trouble finding the fractions. Take turns drawing a card, creating the fraction, and finding its equivalent fraction so that your child can see you model how to do it.

4 Fraction/Decimal Concentration

TIME: 15–20 minutes

MATERIALS
- 24 index cards
- crayons or markers

On six index cards, write a decimal to the tens place. On another six index cards, write the equivalent fractions. On six more index cards, write a decimal to the hundreds place. On the last six cards, write the equivalent fractions. For example, you could write the following:

Decimals to tens place	0.1	0.5	0.6	0.7	0.8	0.3
Equivalent fractions	$^1/_{10}$	$^5/_{10}$	$^6/_{10}$	$^7/_{10}$	$^8/_{10}$	$^3/_{10}$
Decimals to hundreds place	0.01	0.50	0.06	0.24	0.63	0.95
Equivalent fractions	$^1/_{100}$	$^{50}/_{100}$	$^6/_{100}$	$^{24}/_{100}$	$^{63}/_{100}$	$^{95}/_{100}$

After you have written 12 decimals and 12 equivalent fractions on the index cards, shuffle the cards and place them facedown in a grid pattern (three rows, with four cards in each row).

Learning happens when: the first player turns over two cards, looking for a match (the decimal card with its equivalent fraction card). If the player matches the two cards, she takes the cards and goes again. The player's turn ends when she picks two cards that do not match. If the player's cards do not match, the cards are returned to their places and it is the other player's turn. Play continues until all cards have been matched. The players count the cards, and the person with the most cards wins.

Variations: Once your child is successful with these cards, you can make a set of more difficult cards.

- Movers and shakers will learn through hunting for pairs.
- Visual learners should get reinforcement through putting pairs side by side, so they can see the cards that are related.
- Auditory learners will get extra reinforcement by reading the fraction and decimal cards aloud.

Mastery occurs when: your child knows which cards are matches.

You may want to help your child a little more if: she is having trouble finding matching cards. Make a set of cards that have fractions and decimals only in the tens place. Once your child understands how those cards relate, make another set that has fractions and decimals only in the hundreds place. Once she understands how that set works, then introduce a set that mixes tens and hundreds.

5 | What's My Rule?

Learning happens when: you tell your child it's time to play What's My Rule? Think of a rule, such as "multiply by two." This is the input number. Don't tell your child what the rule is. Ask him for a number. You apply the rule mentally and give your child the output number. For example, if your child says, "Five," you mentally multiply by two and tell your child, "Ten." He then gives you another number, you apply the rule, and give the output number.

TIME: 5 minutes

This continues until your child believes he knows the rule. At that point, you give him a number. He mentally applies the rule he believes is correct and gives you the output number. If he is right, ask your child to tell you the rule in words. If he is incorrect, the play continues. This activity will be difficult at first, but it gets easier with practice.

Variations: Once your child understands how the game works, have him think of the rule, and play so that you are the one trying to determine the rule. Also, you may want to write the rules on index cards and place them at one end of the room. Then have your child search for the correct rule while you time him to see how fast he can bring the correct rule back to you. When it is your turn, have your child time you.

- Movers and shakers will enjoy playing the variation where they get to run to the other end of the room and bring the rule back to you.

- It may help visual learners to write down the input and the output numbers to determine the rule. Try to encourage your child to do it mentally once he is comfortable doing it on paper.

- Auditory learners can verbalize the input numbers and the output numbers. For example, have your child say, "A three goes in and a five comes out."

Mastery occurs when: your child can figure out a rule after three or four numbers.

You may want to help your child a little more if: he is having trouble determining the rule. Start with very simple rules. If your child still has trouble, try doing only addition rules first. Then move on to the other operations as he gets more comfortable.

6 Algebraically Speaking

Prepare the deck by taking out the tens and all the face cards. Make the aces worth one. On the index cards, write the four operation signs and the equal sign $(+, -, \times, \div,$ and $=.)$

TIME: 15–20 minutes

MATERIALS
- deck of cards
- 5 index cards
- alphabet letters (if you do not have plastic or foam letters, you can write each letter on a separate index card)

Learning occurs when: you use the cards and letters to create math sentences that have a variable. (Avoid using the letter x as a variable. This causes a lot of confusion with elementary school students, because the $\times$ is an operation sign.) For example, your sentence may look like this: $7 + b = 12$

Explain to your child that b represents a secret number. It is not just any number, but a specific number that makes the math sentence correct. Your child's task is to find the secret number card. Once she finds the card, have your child take the letter out of the math sentence and put the number card in the sentence. Check to make sure the number makes the math sentence correct. Once your child has found that secret number, make another math sentence. Do several, using different operations and different letters as variables.

Variations: Once your child is comfortable, have her make a math sentence that contains a variable for you to solve.

- Actually taking out the letter and replacing it with a number will help kinesthetic learners understand how variables work.

- Seeing letters in a math sentence will help visual learners be more comfortable with variables.

- Verbalizing the math sentences with and without the variables will reinforce this concept for auditory learners.

Mastery occurs when: your child understands variables and can readily find the number represented by the variable.

You may want to help your child a little more if: she gets confused with letters in the math sentence. Your child has probably been introduced to variables but has not used letters. Many textbooks and workbooks use boxes for unknowns, and students are asked to write the unknown number in the box. Explain to your child that the letters work the same way. Start with simple math sentences she will understand easily. Once she is comfortable working with variables in simple sentences, make them a little more complex.

7 | Pattern Hunt

TIME: 10–15 minutes

MATERIALS
- small notebook
- pencils

Learning occurs when: your child searches the house for patterns. Your house is full of patterns, many of which you do not notice because you see them every day. For example, your child may find patterns in a tiled floor, artwork, clothing, masonry, or landscaping. Challenge your child to find as many patterns as he can. Ask him to describe the patterns he finds in the notebook and then share them with you.

Variations: Ask your child to draw the patterns as well as write them. You may also ask him to pick a pattern he would change and have him draw the new pattern.

- Moving around and searching for patterns will keep the interest of kinesthetic learners.
- Visual learners will do well with the activity and are likely to find patterns in more things than you imagined.
- Auditory learners will benefit from talking to you about the patterns they find.

Mastery occurs when: your child finds patterns in everyday objects.

You may want to help your child a little more if: he has difficulty finding patterns. Work with your child to find patterns in one room. Once he understands what he is looking for, have him work independently.

8 Decimal/Fraction Hunt

Learning occurs when: your child looks for fractions and decimals that are used in real life. Have her look through a magazine or a newspaper, searching for decimals and fractions. When your child finds a fraction or a decimal, discuss with her what it means and why a fraction or decimal was used.

TIME: 10–15 minutes

MATERIALS
▪ magazines and newspapers

Variations: Look for fractions and decimals in places outside the home, such as the grocery store, the mall, or the zoo.

✋ Kinesthetic learners will enjoy the hunt and will benefit from finding decimals and fractions in real life.

👁 Visual learners will benefit from seeing the fractions and decimals in many different places.

👂 Discussing how fractions and decimals are used will help auditory learners.

Mastery occurs when: your child readily finds fractions and decimals in real life and understands why they are used instead of whole numbers.

You may want to help your child a little more if: she is having trouble finding fractions and decimals. Look with her. If you find an example, point your child in the right direction. Also, discuss fractions and decimals with her, especially why they are used instead of whole numbers.

Geometry and Measurement

This year, your child will be looking at lines and angles. Specifically, he or she will be learning to understand, identify, and construct intersecting, parallel, and perpendicular lines.

Here's a quick review of those terms:

- Intersecting lines are lines that cross each other.

- Parallel lines are lines that never cross.

- Perpendicular lines make a 90° angle (a T or an L shape where they meet).

Your child will also explore angles and will identify and compare acute, right, and obtuse angles.

- Acute angles are angles that are less than 90°.

- Right angles are angles that equal 90°.

- Obtuse angles are angles that are greater than 90°.

Your child will be working with a coordinate graph. This is a grid that has four sections (or quadrants) and an *x*-axis (horizontal axis) and a *y*-axis (vertical axis) on which points can be placed that have a horizontal and a vertical value. Your child will be learning to place points on a coordinate graph and name points that are located on a grid or map. In measurement, your child will be learning to establish benchmarks (any standard that something can be measured by, such as inches, meters, and so on). For customary and metric units, he or she will estimate the measures of a variety of objects, select appropriate units to measure things, and solve problems involving perimeter, area, volume, money, time, and temperature.

The table on page 111 describes some skills related to geometry and measurement, where children can run into problems, and what you can do to help them along.

Geometry and Measurement Skills	Having Problems?	Quick Tips
Understands, identifies, and constructs intersecting, parallel, and perpendicular lines.	Has trouble remembering the difference between intersecting, parallel, and perpendicular lines.	To help your child remember that intersecting lines are lines that cross each other, talk to him about intersections, which are places where roads cross each other. Perpendicular lines are a special type of intersecting lines. They cross so that they create four right angles. Perpendicular lines look like a plus sign (+). Parallel lines are two lines that run side by side, never crossing. The two l's in the word "parallel" are an example of parallel lines.
Identifies and compares acute, right, and obtuse angles.	Has trouble remembering the difference between acute, right, and obtuse angles.	Right angles are 90°, like the corners of a box. The angle has to be just right, or the box will not stand straight. Acute angles are angles less than 90°. You can help your child remember an acute angle by suggesting that it's so small that it's cute. Obtuse angles are big (greater than 90°) and funny looking, just like their name.
Knows how to work with a coordinate graph.	Cannot remember in which order to read the ordered pair on a coordinate graph.	The most common problem is forgetting to read the bottom number first (from the x-axis) and then the number on the side (the y-axis). Practice is the best solution. Maps often have a grid, with ordered pairs. Get out a map and ask your child to find the ordered pair for various places on the map.

(continued)

Geometry and Measurement Skills	Having Problems?	Quick Tips
Understands benchmarks for standard and metric units.	Does not know about how much a particular measurement is, for example, how big an inch is.	Benchmarks are common items that help your child remember measurement. For example, to measure length, a benchmark for one centimeter would be the width of your child's little finger. A benchmark for an inch would be the length of your child's pinkie finger. For weight, a paper clip weighs about a gram, and a brick weighs about a kilogram. A large can of green beans weighs about a pound. For volume, an eyedropper can hold about a milliliter of water, and some water bottles hold a liter of water. A gallon of milk is a benchmark most students know. The point is to try to find common items your child can use as benchmarks for measurements.
Can estimate the measurements of a variety of objects.	Cannot estimate the measurements of a variety of objects.	The key is strong benchmarks. Your child must have a good idea of what the measurement is. Benchmarks help your child to internalize them. Once he has some strong benchmarks, estimating the measures of different objects will not be difficult. For example, your child may be asked if a raisin is closer to one gram or one kilogram. If he has benchmarks, such as that a paperclip weighs about 1 gram and a brick weighs about 1 kilogram, he will easily see that a raisin is closer in weight to a gram.

Geometry and Measurement Skills	Having Problems?	Quick Tips
Selects appropriate units to measure things.	Does not know which unit to use to measure objects.	Practice, practice, practice. Get out the tape measure and have your child measure the lengths of many things. Have her cook with you to practice volume measurements. Get a simple pan balance (like the kind used to measure produce) to compare weights.
Understands the differences between perimeter, area, and volume.	Confuses perimeter, area, and volume.	Use a real-world example to help your child remember the differences. One example may be putting in a pool in your backyard. Most cities require that a fence be put around the pool for safety. The fence represents the perimeter of the pool. During the winter, you will probably want to cover the pool. This represents area. Your pool will also hold water. This represents volume. Not only will the water go the length and width of the pool, it will also have a certain depth as well.
Solves problems involving money.	Has trouble working with money.	Generally, kids are fairly proficient with money in math, because it is an example of how we use math every day. The biggest problem is usually computing change. The best solution is to practice. When you go shopping, have your child try to figure out the change before the cashier can.

(continued)

Geometry and Measurement Skills	Having Problems?	Quick Tips
Solves problems involving time.	Has trouble working with time.	There are two main problems dealing with time. The first is reading the time on an analog clock. Digital clocks are common, while analog clocks are becoming more rare. Make sure there is an analog clock somewhere in your home. Ask your child to read the analog clock daily. The second problem is figuring elapsed time. Having your child help with scheduling issues that will reinforce these concepts. For example, soccer practice starts at 4:15. It lasts for an hour. What time will it be over?
Solves problems involving temperature.	Has trouble working with temperature.	Have your child watch the weather report with you, or turn on the oven when you need it set to a certain temperature. Doing these activities will give your child a sense of the various temperatures during different times of the year as well as the temperatures used in baking.

Geometry and Measurement Activities

 **Line Art**

Learning happens when: your child uses the ruler, a pencil, and the paper to create a picture that is composed only of straight line segments. Make sure your child uses some parallel lines, some intersecting lines, and some perpendicular lines. The picture can be anything—real or abstract. After he is satisfied with the picture, ask him to find and highlight the different types of lines. Pick one of the highlighters (yellow, for example) to highlight perpendicular lines, another (blue, for example) to highlight parallel lines, and a third (green, for example) to highlight the intersecting lines.

Variations: You can draw a picture made entirely of line segments and have your child find and highlight examples of the different types of lines.

✋ Kinesthetic learners will enjoy using the ruler to create the lines.

👁 Visual learners will probably find the different types of lines fairly quickly.

👂 Have auditory learners say why the different lines fit the different categories as they are highlighting them.

Mastery occurs when: your child understands the different types of lines and can find examples for each of them.

You may want to help your child a little more if: he is having difficulty understanding the different types of lines. Find one example with your child and ask him to find two more examples of the same type of line. Do the same thing for the other types of lines.

2 | Angle Search

Learning occurs when: you and your child search through the magazines to find examples of the different types of angles. Label one of the sheets of construction paper "Right Angles." (Remember, right angles are exactly 90° and look like the corners of a square or a rectangle.) Label another sheet of construction paper "Acute Angles." (Acute angles are less than 90° and look like a right angle that has been closed.) Label the third sheet of

TIME: 10–15 minutes

MATERIALS
- ruler
- pencils
- white construction paper
- 3 highlighters of different colors

TIME: 20–30 minutes

MATERIALS
- magazines
- 3 large sheets of construction paper
- crayons or markers
- rounded-edge scissors
- nontoxic glue

construction paper "Obtuse Angles." (Obtuse angles are larger than 90°. They look like a right angle that has been opened up.) After the papers are labeled, you and your child should go through the magazines to find and cut out examples of angles. For this activity, an angle does not necessarily have to be made of line segments. An angle can be created by the bend of a person's arm, in the lines created by the roof line of a building, and so on. When you have several angles cut out, categorize them by placing them on the pieces of construction paper according to the type of angle. If you notice that you do not have very many of a particular type of angle, search the magazines again, looking only for that type of angle. When you are satisfied that you have all the examples in the correct categories, glue the angles to the appropriate sheet of paper.

Variations: If your child is the competitive type, you can have a race to see who can find the most of a particular type of angle. Each of you should have a magazine and a pair of scissors. Set a timer for five minutes. When you say go, both of you will search the magazines for one particular type of angle. When the time is up, count how many each of you has found. Score one point for each correct type found and deduct one point for any angles that are not of the type for which you were searching. Do the same for the other types of angles.

✋ Cutting out the angles will help kinesthetic learners internalize the different types.

👁 Visual learners will benefit from seeing the product of this activity. Each of the sheets of paper will be like a miniposter for the types of angles.

👂 For auditory learners, be sure to discuss what you are doing as you categorize the angles.

Mastery occurs when: your child knows the different types of angles and can find examples of each.

You may want to help your child a little more if: she is having trouble finding angles. Search together. Ask her to first find pictures that have some sort of straight lines in them. Where two lines cross, four angles are created. Your child can pick one of the four angles to cut out. First look only for one type of angle. Once your child understands that type of angle, move on to another. Continue until she understands all three types.

3 | Lines and Angles Concentration

On six of the cards, write one of the following: "intersecting lines," "parallel lines," "perpendicular lines," "right angle," "acute angle," and "obtuse angle." On the other six cards, draw a picture or glue a picture of the following: two lines that intersect to form an x; two lines that intersect to form a plus sign (+); two parallel lines; a right angle; an acute angle; and an obtuse angle.

TIME: 10–15 minutes

MATERIALS
- 12 index cards
- markers or crayons

Learning occurs when: your child matches the name of a type of line or angle with a picture of that type of line or angle. Explain to your child that the intersecting lines card goes with the card that looks like an x and the perpendicular lines card goes with the card that looks like the plus sign. Shuffle the cards and place them facedown in a 3 × 4 grid. One player turns over two cards. If the name matches the picture, the player keeps both cards. If there is no match, the cards are again placed facedown and it's the other player's turn. Continue playing until all matches have been made. The person who collects the most cards wins.

Variations: Have your child create the cards himself.

✋ Movers and shakers enjoy games that require them to physically do something. The act of flipping the cards over and remembering the placement of the cards will benefit kinesthetic learners.

👁 Visual learners will receive reinforcement by linking the word with a picture.

👂 Auditory learners may need to verbalize why a picture does or does not match the word card.

Mastery occurs when: your child can quickly tell whether the picture card matches the word card.

You may want to help your child a little more if: he is having difficulty making the matches. Play the game faceup until your child can quickly match the picture to the name. When your child can match them fairly easily, begin by playing the traditional method.

4 | Race to a Meter

Time: 20–30 minutes

Materials
- paper a little longer than 1 meter
- colored pencils
- metric ruler
- die

Learning occurs when: you and your child play a game that requires measurement. Lay out the paper on a work surface. Draw a line at one end of the paper to represent the starting line. Draw a second line at the other end of the paper that is 1 meter from the starting line. Decide who will go first. Player 1 rolls the die. The number rolled represents how many centimeters long player 1's line will be. For example, if player 1 rolls a five, she will put one end of the ruler at the starting point, draw a dot at the 5-centimeter mark, and draw a line connecting the starting point to the dot. Player 2 then rolls the die and uses that number to determine how long a line to draw from the starting point. Play continues with each player adding onto her line until one player's line crosses the finish line.

Variations: This same game can be played as a race to a yard, drawing lines in increments of inches.

✋ Kinesthetic learners will enjoy the movement involved in measuring and will better retain the length of a centimeter and a meter.

👁 Visual learners will benefit from seeing how long the various lines are and the length of 1 meter.

👂 Auditory learners will benefit from thinking aloud as they complete the game.

Mastery occurs when: your child can draw a line the correct length, according to the number rolled, and understands the lengths of a centimeter and a meter.

You may want to help your child a little more if: she is having trouble with the game. Completing the game with her will help because you are there for instant feedback and will model for your child how to correctly measure a line of a certain length.

5 | A Weighty Matter in the Kitchen

Label one sheet of paper "Exactly 1 Pound," the second sheet "More Than 1 Pound," and the last sheet "Less Than 1 Pound."

Learning occurs when: your child finds and weighs items to determine if they are exactly 1 pound, more than 1 pound, or less than 1 pound. Place your item that weighs 1 pound on one side of the balance scale. Have your child place a box, a bag, or a can of food from the pantry on the other side. If the scale is balanced, the item weighs exactly 1 pound. If the scale tips toward the item weighing 1 pound, the item weighs less than a pound. If the scale tips toward the item your child placed on the scale, the item weighs

TIME: 20–30 minutes

MATERIALS
- pencils
- balance scale
- 3 pieces of paper
- something that weighs exactly 1 pound
- items from your kitchen pantry

more than a pound. Have your child weigh several things and place them on the correct piece of paper. After several items have been compared, have your child look at the items that are on each piece of paper. Have your child look at the labels on the boxes, bags, and cans of food for the actual weight. See if your child can determine how many ounces are in a pound by weighing items and looking at their labels.

Variations: You can do the same thing with grams and kilograms. It will be more difficult to find something that weighs exactly 1 kilogram, but if you find it, this activity will be fairly simple.

- Kinesthetic learners will enjoy using the balance scale to understand weight.
- Watching how the balance scale works and seeing the items categorized will help visual learners.
- Auditory learners may need to think aloud as they are weighing and categorizing.

Mastery occurs when: your child has a sense of how much a pound is and can use the scale to determine if an item is more or less than a pound.

You may want to help your child a little more if: he is having difficulty completing the task. Weigh a few items with him until your child is comfortable with the task.

Data Analysis and Probability

Data analysis is a huge concept for your child, because it is one that spans many different subjects. Your child will be expected to read and understand charts, tables, and graphs in math, reading, social studies, and science. In math, she will be asked to examine data displays such as tallies, tables, charts, and graphs. In addition, she will then use her observations about the data to pose and answer questions. Your child will also be asked to collect, organize, and record data in tables and graphs. Probability is an area in which she will be building on information learned in previous years. Your child will investigate and record probabilities by experimenting with devices that generate random outcomes, such as coins, number cubes, and spinners.

The following table describes some skills related to data analysis and probability, where children can run into problems, and what you can do to help them along.

Data Analysis and Probability Skills	Having Problems?	Quick Tips
Examines data displays and uses observations to pose and answer questions.	Has trouble reading data displays, such as tallies, tables, charts, and graphs.	Have your child help you read data displays in everyday life. For example, ask your child to help read his soccer schedule. Play games that require him to keep track of things by using tally marks.
Collects, organizes, and records data in tables and graphs.	Has trouble collecting and organizing information.	Start by having your child keep track of her activities on a calendar. Have her help you do tasks, such as inventory your books, movies, or CDs.
Investigates and records probabilities by experimenting with devices that generate random outcomes.	Does not understand how probability relates to coins, number cubes, and spinners.	Real-life experience will help your child understand these concepts. Yahtzee is a great probability game. Higher points are awarded to dice combinations that are statistically more difficult to get. Play games that have spinners.

Data Analysis and Probability Activities

1 | Quiz Maker

TIME: 20–30 minutes

MATERIALS

social studies textbook
(or any source that has
kid-friendly tables, charts,
and graphs)

paper

pencils

Learning occurs when: your child answers questions about a table, graph, or chart and then creates questions about another table, graph, or chart. Find a chart and create four or five questions about the chart. Have him answer the questions by looking at the chart. After he has answered the questions, have him find another graph, table, or chart and create four or five questions for you to answer. Your child should make an answer key to go with his questions. After you have answered the questions, have him check your answers. Discuss with your child your answers and how they compare to the answer key he created. You can learn a lot about your child's level of understanding based on his questions and answers.

Variations: Create a game. You and your child will each individually create four or five questions about several different charts, graphs, and tables. Then each will take turns asking your questions. A correct answer scores a point. An incorrect answer deducts a point. The person with the most points at the end of the game wins.

Your kinesthetic learner will enjoy standing up and "teaching" you about the chart as he asks the questions. Let your learner present the chart to you and point out features of it when you need a "hint" to answer the question.

Visual learners should react well to this activity because of the visual nature of data displays.

Your auditory learner will benefit from discussing the questions with you.

Mastery occurs when: your child can look at a data display, answer questions about it, and create questions about it.

You may want to help your child a little more if: he is having trouble answering the questions. Make your questions very basic at first. Go over the organization of the data display with your child before asking the questions. As his confidence grows, make the questions a little tougher. Do not have your child create questions until he is comfortable with answering questions about the chart.

2 | Transferring Data

Learning occurs when: your child takes information from one source and transfers it to another. The schedule can be for sports, school, important dates to remember, and so forth. Have your child look at the schedule and write the information on a calendar.

TIME: 10–15 minutes

MATERIALS
any type of schedule
calendar

Variations: If your child loves to organize, have her take multiple schedules and put them on a master calendar, color-coding the activities of various family members.

- Kinesthetic learners will enjoy actually moving the data from one source to another. Post the master calendar on a wall and give your child different colors to write with.
- Visual learners will benefit from seeing their activities organized in one place.
- Discuss your auditory learner's calendar with her in detail. She may benefit from talking with you about the upcoming day at the same time each morning or evening.

Mastery occurs when: your child can take data from one source and accurately put it on a calendar.

You may want to help your child a little more if: she is having difficulty transferring the data. Do a few with your child first. When she understands how to complete the task, let her do it independently.

3 | How Many Commercials?

TIME: 20–30 minutes

MATERIALS
- paper
- pencils

Learning happens when: your child keeps track of how many commercials occur during several television shows and graphs the results. Have your child pick four to five television shows to analyze. Make sure that each show is on for the same length of time. Record what time of day or night the show is on and what day of the week. These pieces of information provide the context for the rest of the information your child gathers. He will watch each of the shows and keep a tally of the number of commercials that are aired during that show. After your child has all his data, he should put the data in a graph form that will be easy to read. Ask your child to present the information to you. Discuss things like what kind of commercials are on during certain times of the day or week and what kind of commercials are on during which shows. Who do the people who made the commercials want to watch the advertisements? Do advertisers of the same types of products have different types of commercials for different shows? There are many things to discuss about the information your child has gathered.

Variations: Your child can keep track of the different types of commercials that are aired during four or five of his favorite shows. For example, how many are food commercials? How many are toy commercials?

👋 Kinesthetic learners will enjoy adding a special game of charades to this activity. After you discuss the information your child recorded about commercials, say the time of day and/or week and ask your child to act out a type of commercial that would be aired at that time.

👁 Visual learners will benefit from seeing their data organized visually.

👂 Your auditory child will benefit from discussing and recording information about what he heard, such as the type of music in the commercials and the way the narrator is talking.

Mastery occurs when: your child can collect the data, organize it, and present it in an easy-to-read graph.

You may want to help your child a little more if: he is having trouble completing this task. Make sure your child knows how to keep tally marks. You also may need to make sure he remembers the task. Getting very involved in the television show may make it difficult for him to remember to keep track of the commercials. If your child is having trouble organizing and presenting the data, guide him at first. Ask him what information needs to be included. How can the information be organized so someone can quickly understand the data?

4 | My Music Collection

Learning happens when: your child categorizes her music collection and presents her findings in a data display. The first step is to have your child decide how she will categorize the music. It can be by genre (pop, R&B, country, classical, soundtracks, etc.), or it can be by singer—male versus female, groups versus solo artists, and so forth. There is no end to how she can categorize the collection. After your child has decided how she will categorize the collection, she will gather data. Have your child go through

TIME: 20–30 minutes

MATERIALS
paper
pencils

the collection and keep a tally according to category. After she has categorized the collection, she will need to present the data in an organized, easy-to-read graph format.

Variations: Do the same activity with a movie collection, books, and so on.

✍ Kinesthetic learners will appreciate the hands-on activity of digging through their collection. Once they have decided on their categories, it will help them to physically move the items into groups by category before graphing the data.

👁 Visual learners will be especially good at presenting their results in a very organized way.

🎧 Auditory learners should discuss their results before presenting them in a graph, and they might want to present the information to you using the graph as a visual aid.

Mastery occurs when: your child can gather the data, organize it, and present it in some graphic way.

You may want to help your child a little more if: she is overwhelmed with this project. Break it down into manageable chunks. Have her categorize part of the collection and present the results.

5 | Coin Probabilities

Time: 10 minutes

Materials
- 2 different coins
- paper
- pencils

Learning occurs when: your child determines the probability of outcomes by flipping two coins and then performing an experiment to test the probability. Start with a penny and a dime, for example. Have your child figure out how many different ways these coins could land if they are flipped. The following are the combinations:

Penny	Dime
Heads	Heads
Heads	Tails
Tails	Heads
Tails	Tails

Probability is expressed as a fraction. The probability of flipping two heads is ¼. The table shows this. Out of four possible outcomes, only one possibility is two heads. The probability of flipping two tails is ¼. Out of four possible outcomes, only one possibility is two tails. However, the probability of flipping one head and one tail is ²⁄₄. Out of four possible outcomes, two possibilities are the heads/tails combination. This is the same as ½. This is a tough concept, and you may need to discuss this with your child. Once he understands the probabilities, have him flip the penny and the dime 100 times, keeping a tally of how many times the coins land heads/heads, heads/tails, or tails/tails. You may want to tally for your child while he flips the coins and then trade jobs. See if approximately half of the time the coins land heads/tails. Heads/heads and tails/tails should occur only about half as often as heads/tails.

Variations: If your child loves this activity, try it with three different coin combinations.

🖐 Kinesthetic learners will appreciate being able to flip the coins.

👁 Have visual learners put the tally results in a graph format.

👂 Have auditory learners call out the results of each coin flip and read the final tallies aloud.

Mastery occurs when: your child makes the connection between the outcomes and why some outcomes will occur more often than others.

You may want to help your child a little more if: he is having trouble understanding the difference in probabilities. Make sure you use different coins and do the same process to show that the outcome stays the same. Discuss this again with your child using the table to support your explanation. This is a tough concept, and you may need to come back to it later if your child just does not understand.

6 Summing Up the Dice

TIME: 20 minutes

MATERIALS
- 2 dice
- pencils
- lined paper

Learning occurs when: your child writes the numbers 2 through 12 on different lines on the paper. These are the possible sums of two dice. Your child's task is to roll the two dice, add the numbers together, and make tally marks of the sums. The task ends when one number gets twenty tally marks. One of the sums should show up more than any of the others. Challenge your child to figure out why that number occurred most often. If her results match what statistically should have happened, seven will occur most often, while two and twelve will occur least often, because there is only one way to get two $(1 + 1)$ and one way to get twelve $(6 + 6)$. There are two ways to get three $(1 + 2, 2 + 1)$ and eleven $(5 + 6, 6 + 5)$. There are three ways to get four $(1 + 3, 2 + 2, 3 + 1)$ and ten $(4 + 6, 5 + 5, 6 + 4)$. There are four ways to get five $(1 + 4, 2 + 3, 3 + 2, 4 + 1)$ and nine $(3 + 6, 4 + 5, 5 + 4, 6 + 3)$. There are five ways to get six $(1 + 5, 2 + 4, 3 + 3, 4 + 2, 5 + 1)$ and eight $(2 + 6, 3 + 5, 4 + 4, 5 + 3, 6 + 2)$. Finally, there are six ways to get seven $(1 + 6, 2 + 5, 3 + 4, 4 + 3, 5 + 2, 6 + 1)$. Seven may not get the most tallies for your child, but it should have nearly the most. If another number occurs most often, explain that probability shows what *should* happen, but it does not guarantee that it *will* happen.

Variations: You can extend this activity by having your child graph her results.

- 👋 Kinesthetic learners will enjoy working with the dice.
- 👁 Visual learners will appreciate seeing the data organized in tallies and may want to extend it by graphing their results.
- 👂 Have auditory learners call out the results of each roll of the dice and read the final tallies aloud.

Mastery occurs when: your child understands why seven should occur most often and can keep her data organized.

You may want to help your child a little more if: she is having difficulty understanding why seven should occur most often. Draw a T-table, with the headings of "Die #1" and "Die #2." Go over with your child how two dice will make 12. Then ask your child to tell you how to make 11. Ask her if there's any other way. At first, your child probably will not see 5 + 6 as being different from 6 + 5. Explain that there are two different dice, and 5 + 6 has die #1 getting a 5 and die #2 getting a 6, while 6 + 5 has die #1 getting a 6 and die #2 getting a 5. Your child will probably understand in those terms.

7 Time and Temp

Make a table for time, temperature, and days of the week, like the one on page 130.

Calculate the average temperature for one week.

Learning happens when: your child learns to read a thermometer and record the data in the correct manner. Also, math skills are

TIME: 1 time period in the day (30 minutes each) at the same time of day for one week

MATERIALS
▢ 1 piece of paper
▢ 1 large clock
▢ 1 large outdoor thermometer

	Time	**Temperature in °F**
Sunday		
Monday		
Tuesday		
Wednesday		
Thursday		
Friday		
Saturday		

incorporated when the child adds all the temperatures and divides by 7 to get an average.

Variations: Your child can do the same activity by recording the data for temperature in degrees Celsius and determine the differences in the two systems.

✋ Kinesthetic learners will enjoy going outside and handling the equipment.

👁 Visual learners like watching the clock and the thermometer and recording the data.

👂 Auditory learners may need to announce their findings and ask you for questions.

Mastery occurs when: your child has a sense of time and temperature and what average numbers mean.

You may want to help your child a little more if: he is having trouble calculating the average temperature. Try helping your child average two days' temperatures before trying to average a whole week's worth of data.

8 | Perimeter and Area

Find an area outside that has weeds (like dandelions) or rocks. Place the sticks in the ground in the shape of a 40 × 40-inch square. Tie the cord to the sticks or use thumbtacks to attach the cord. Have your child get inside the roped-off area and count the number of dandelions or rocks within the area. Have her determine the perimeter and the area of the roped-off ground. Ask how many dandelions or rocks she found in the population sample.

Learning happens when: your child calculates the perimeter and the area and realizes that population samples for anything is similar to this activity. Learning also occurs when your child records data and constructs the sample area. She also adds a new word, *population*, to her vocabulary.

Variations: Your child can do this activity by measuring a room in the house and counting the pieces of furniture in the room.

✋ Kinesthetic learners enjoy using the tape measure, attaching the string, and moving around.

👁 Visual learners like to see the finished product and how the tape measure is numbered.

👂 Auditory learners like to hear the instructions and think about how they will build the area.

Mastery occurs when: your child is able to measure and calculate mathematically perimeter and area, and understands oral or written directions on building the project.

You may want to help your child a little more if: she is having trouble measuring the perimeter and then calculating the area. Try measuring the perimeter twice—once with your child and then

TIME: 20 minutes

MATERIALS
▪ 4 sticks 24 inches tall to stick in the ground
▪ roll of white twine or cord (cut to 160 inches)
▪ thumbtacks
▪ tape measure
▪ paper
▪ pencils

once with your child measuring on her own. This is a good time to teach the adage "measure twice, cut once"—it will make your child feel like you are working together and not like you are there to make sure she does it right, and it is a good habit to get into at an early age (measuring twice). Compare your answers to see if they are the same; if they are not, measure again. If calculating is where your child is stumbling, set up the problem for her and then let her work out the answer.

9 Fair or Unfair?

TIME: 20 minutes

MATERIALS
▪ various spinners

Learning occurs when: your child examines spinners to determine if they are fair or unfair. Fair spinners are those in which each outcome has an equal chance of occurring. An unfair spinner does not have equal parts. Raid the games in your house for spinners. Discuss with your child what a fair and an unfair spinner is. Examine the spinner. Is it fair or unfair? If it is unfair, what are you most likely to spin? What are you least likely to spin? Once your child understands the concept of fair and unfair, have him design a spinner that has three prizes on it. The challenge is to create a spinner that will increase the chance that your child will win the prize he most desires. Your child's spinner simply needs to be designed so that his desired prize has the largest portion of the spinner. You can have your child draw the spinner on paper, cut it out, and put it over the bottom of a spinner from one of his games.

Variations: Have your child make up a game that uses a spinner. It can be an unfair spinner or a fair one. You may be surprised at what your child creates.

Kinesthetic learners will appreciate being able to play with the spinner.

👁 Visual learners will benefit from designing their own spinners.

👂 Auditory learners will benefit most from the discussion with you about fair and unfair spinners. They should also call out the answers the spinners land on.

Mastery occurs when: your child understands the difference between fair and unfair spinners.

You may want to help your child a little more if: he is having difficulty with this concept. Make sure your child can look at a spinner and tell if the sections are equal.

Environmental Learning

Math is a great subject to cover in everyday life. Just handling money, for example, can teach all forms of operations—addition, subtraction, multiplication, and division—as well as place value and decimals (cents), fractions (four quarters of a dollar), regrouping, and variables. Geometry and measuring are just as easy to find in everyday life. For example, pool is a game of angles. And everything in life is measured— from quantity to length, from temperature to wind speed. There are tons of opportunities to talk about measurement on any given day.

End of Fourth Grade Math Checklist

Students who are working at the standard level at the end of fourth grade:

____ Discover, describe, and extend geometric and number patterns

____ Solve simple math sentences that contain a variable

____ Read, write, and rename whole numbers through the millions

____ Read, write, and rename decimals to the hundreds

____ Compare and order whole numbers and decimals

____ Explore equivalent and nonequivalent fractions and begin to compare, add, and subtract them

____ Multiply larger numbers

____ Have learned long division

____ Begin developing mental math ability and estimation skills

____ Know the basic characteristics of lines and angles

____ Have established measurement benchmarks

____ Can collect, record, and analyze data to investigate probability

Fourth Grade Science 8

Fourth grade science builds on what was studied in the third grade and can be divided into two broad categories: processes and concepts. Science processes include observing and measuring objects, organisms, and/or events; classifying objects, organisms, and/or events using two or more observable properties; arranging items in serial order (for example, least to greatest or fastest to slowest); planning and conducting a science experiment; using a hypothesis; interpreting graphs, charts, and tables; and communicating the results of a science experiment. Science concepts your child will learn this year include how the position and motion of an object can be changed by pushing or pulling; how motion can be described by tracing and measuring; how the flow of electricity is controlled by open and closed circuits and the role of conductors and insulators; the adaptive characteristics of organisms, how organisms can be classified, and the roles

---

Beginning of Fourth Grade Science Checklist

Students who are working at the standard level at the beginning of fourth grade:

_____ Observe, record, and communicate changes

_____ Measure length in centimeters, mass in grams, and temperature in degrees Celsius

_____ Classify objects and organisms

_____ Understand systems and subsystems

_____ Can explain how sound is produced and travels

_____ Know the characteristics, basic needs, and habitats of organisms

_____ Know how organisms fit together in a food chain

_____ Understand how forces such as earthquakes, glaciers, volcanoes, and erosion change the earth

of organisms in a living system; inherited traits versus learned traits; the processes of erosion, weathering, and sedimentation; and fossils as evidence about plants and animals that lived long ago.

Science Processes

Your child will be learning processes in science that will help him in other subjects. One of the biggest processes is observation. Encourage your child to notice things and to pay attention to the world around him. Observation is the first step in the scientific method. Being able to read different types of charts, graphs, and tables is a skill that is found across all subjects—math, reading, social studies, and science. It is a very important skill to have. Your child will also be comparing and contrasting characteristics of objects, organisms, and/or events, such as by color, shape, size, texture, sound, position, and change. As an extension, your child will be asked to classify items according to two or more observable properties. He will be asked to arrange items and/or organisms in serial order from least to greatest or fastest to slowest. Finally, your child will be conducting experiments, using the scientific method. This method includes four well-defined steps:

1. Observation. Your child needs to notice something she wants to test or create an experiment about.

2. Hypothesis. After your child notices something, she will formulate a hypothesis, which is simply a prediction about what will happen when your child performs the experiment.

3. Experiment. Your child will perform an experiment and then look at the results to see if the hypothesis is supported or not supported.

4. Report. Your child will communicate her results through writing and graphs, as well as possibly illustrations or photographs.

The following table describes some skills related to science processes, where children can run into problems, and what you can do to help them along.

Science Process Skills	Having Problems?	Quick Tips
Describes details of things he sees.	Doesn't notice discreet details of things he sees.	Try playing the game "I spy" with your child, choosing small details of an object to spy rather than an object itself.
Follows the scientific method.	Skips steps in the scientific method or does them out of order.	Play follow the leader. Take any activity with sequential steps, such as baking cookies or playing a game, and try to start in the middle. Does that work well? Of course not. Talk about why doing the steps in order is important.

Science Processes Activities

1 Quick Lists

Learning occurs when: your child is given a category and must generate a list of things that fit into the category in a certain amount of time. Categories you could use include: things that are cold, things that live in the water, things that are blue, things that move, people who work with their hands, or things that have four legs. Give your child the category and set the timer for three minutes. Your child should tell you as many things as he can think of that fit in the category before the time is up. Make a note of how many things your child fit into the list; then try another list to see if he can beat his previous record.

TIME: 10–15 minutes

MATERIALS
timer

Variations: You and your child can take turns thinking of categories. Once the category has been selected, your child can say one thing that fits into the category, and then you say another thing that fits into the category. Continue taking turns until neither can think of another item. By taking turns, you and your child can piggyback off each other's ideas and think of more items than neither you nor he could have thought of on your own.

✋ Kinesthetic learners would enjoy a physical element to this activity. Instead of keeping score with points, have your child keep score with movement. Do this activity outdoors. For each correct answer, your child takes one big step forward. See how far he can travel across the yard.

👁 Visual learners may want to write down and keep lists of their items. See how long the lists can grow.

👂 Auditory learners will benefit from saying their lists aloud and may want to discuss why they put certain things on each list.

Mastery occurs when: your child can think of a series of items that fit into a category.

You may want to help your child a little more if: he is having trouble thinking of items. If you use the variation, your child should learn how to complete the activity and get ideas from the things you say.

2 Double Classification

TIME: 10–15 minutes

MATERIALS
- 6 index cards
- crayons or markers

Using the marker, write the following words on the six index cards: "soft," "edible," "white," "alive," "small," and "round."

Learning occurs when: your child thinks of an item or items that can fit into two different categories. Shuffle the cards and place them facedown. Your child will draw two cards and think of as many things as possible that fit the two categories. For example, if she draws "small" and "white," she may think of things such as a snowflake, a marshmallow, or a grain of rice. Count how many items your child listed. Then you take two index cards and think of as many things as possible that fit the two categories. Whoever thought of the most items for the categories wins the round. Put the cards back in the deck, shuffle, and play another round. The person who wins the most rounds out of three wins the game.

Variations: Draw two cards, then take turns listing items that fit both categories. Continue listing items until someone cannot think of another item. Repeat with the rest of the cards. If your child likes competition, keep track of how many items each person listed. The one who thinks of the largest number of items wins.

🖐 For the kinesthetic learner, have a bowl filled with small items such as dried beans, cereal with a hole in the center, colored candies, poker chips, and so on. As your child lists an item, have her take one of the items. See how many items she can collect. Edible items may be eaten at the end of the game, if you wish.

👁 Visual learners may enjoy completing this the same way as kinesthetic learners, seeing how large their pile of items can get. Alternatively, they may want to keep a written list.

👂 Auditory learners will benefit from saying their items aloud and hearing you list your items.

Mastery occurs when: your child can think of several things that fit two categories.

You may want to help your child a little more if: she is having trouble thinking of items that fit into two categories. Take turns listing items. Your child will get ideas from your ideas.

3 | Data Hunt

TIME: 20–30 minutes

MATERIALS
- newspapers
- magazines

Learning occurs when: you have your child look for tables, charts, and graphs in newspapers and magazines and discuss them with him. Ask him to tell you the purpose of each graph. What information is it trying to communicate? Why do we even have charts, tables, and graphs? It is important that your child realizes that the purpose of graphs is to organize and communicate information quickly and clearly.

Variations: Make your own charts that display information about your child and his activities. Track things like how many chores are done each week and the time associated with doing them. You can collect data about homework and after-school activities. Girls may enjoy making a chart about what clothes they wore to school (colors, type, outfits, etc.). When you have a few charts of information about your child, talk about that information. Does it present an easy way for your child to think about how he spends his time, or can he see any patterns in the information?

✍ Kinesthetic learners may need to point to bars on a bar graph, tracing them with their fingers to see which bar is highest. Tracing the slices in a pie graph or the line in a line graph may also give your kinesthetic learner a better sense of which parts of the graph hold the most weight.

👁 The visual clues provided by a table or a graph will help visual learners understand the information much better than words alone.

👂 Auditory learners may need to discuss the graphs with you.

Mastery occurs when: your child can tell you what information the chart, graph, or table is trying to convey.

You may want to help your child a little more if: he is having trouble understanding the graph. A graph from a newspaper or a magazine could easily be about something with which your child has had no experience. Make sure the graph shows information about which your child has some knowledge. For example, graphs about popular culture or sports probably will appeal to your child more than graphs about the political beliefs of various groups.

4 | Double Animal Classification

TIME: 15–20 minutes

MATERIALS
▪ magazines with pictures of animals (or you can purchase ready-made animal cards)
▪ rounded-edge scissors
▪ nontoxic glue
▪ index cards

Learning occurs when: your child classifies animals, using two different categories. If you don't have ready-made animal cards, your child should go through the magazines, cut out pictures of animals, and glue them to index cards. Your child's task is to classify the animals, using two different categories, such as "furry" and "large," or "mammal" and "can hop." After she has classified the animals and has explained the classifications to you, ask her to classify the animals using three different categories. Continue to see in how many ways your child can classify the animals.

Variations: Think of two categories but don't tell your child what they are. Pull only those animal cards that fit the two categories and see if your child can think of the two things they all have in common.

✋ Have your kinesthetic learner put on a paper plate all the cards that fit into one category. Then, have her pull from the paper plate only the cards that fit the second category. This will ensure that the cards fit both categories.

👁 Allow your visual learner to lay out all the cards faceup so she can look at all the cards while categorizing.

👂 Auditory learners may need to think aloud as they classify the animals.

Mastery occurs when: your child can classify the animals using two characteristics.

You may want to help your child a little more if: she is having trouble understanding how to classify the animals. Try the kinesthetic approach, having your child classify the first category before moving on to the second.

5 -Est Animals

TIME: 20–30 minutes

MATERIALS
▪ animal cards or a reference source such as an encyclopedia or a Web site
▪ paper
▪ pencils

Learning occurs when: your child puts animals in serial order according to a shared characteristic. A set of animal cards may have the information needed to complete this activity. If not, your child may need to do some research. Have your child pick five animals that he will use. Pick a category, such as weight, running speed, size, life span, or amount of food eaten and give the paper a title. Your child will then write down the names of the animals on the paper in serial order, from greatest to least. Then have your child list the data that prove the animals are in the correct order.

Variations: Have your child create some awards, such as Speedy Award, Award for Eating the Most Food, or Award for Weighing the Most. Your child will research which animal should win the various awards.

✋ Kinesthetic learners may enjoy researching on the Internet, but make sure they stay on task.

👁 Visual learners will benefit from having the pictures of each animal available and may want to include pictures in their list of animals.

Auditory learners may want to present the information orally.

Mastery occurs when: your child can put animals in serial order, according to a given category.

You may want to help your child a little more if: he is having trouble with this activity. Make a T-chart to help your child keep the information organized. List the animals in one column and information about a particular category in the other column. Once the T-chart is filled in, your child should find it fairly simple to rank the animals.

6 Real Experiments

Learning occurs when: you make an "I wonder . . ." statement to your child, such as, "I wonder what will happen if I don't water this plant that was grown from a seed." Make sure the statement is something that can be safely tested. Once you have made the statement, you and your child will design an experiment to see what will happen. The first thing to do is to make a hypothesis. Ask your child to predict what will happen. Your child may say, "The plant will wilt." That prediction is the hypothesis. So, your child's hypothesis would be, "A plant that is not watered will wilt." Have your child write her hypothesis on the paper. The next step is to design how the hypothesis will be tested. Make sure your child is very detailed and specific. Instead of saying, "I will not water the plant," your child should say, "I will not water the plant for two weeks. On every Tuesday and Thursday, I will look at the plant and write down the observations I make." Have your child write down the steps of the experiment on the paper after the hypothesis. Since the example says your child will write down her observations every Tuesday and Thursday, have her do so on the

TIME: 30 minutes

MATERIALS
- plant grown from a seed
- paper
- pencils

paper. At the end of the two weeks, your child will see whether her hypothesis has been supported. Your child may want to experiment further, based on her results. Once the experiment is over, have your child communicate her results by presenting the data in an organized way, such as in a table and/or graph.

Variations: Your child can experiment on any number of things depending on her interests.

✍ Science experiments generally appeal to kinesthetic learners because of the hands-on discovery learning that occurs.

👁 Visual learners will enjoy communicating their results in tables and graphs and may also want to include drawings or pictures of their experiment.

👂 Auditory learners may need to discuss the steps as they complete the experiment.

Mastery occurs when: your child understands how to make a hypothesis, design an experiment, conduct an experiment, and communicate the results.

You may want to help your child a little more if: she seems overwhelmed. There are so many parts to this activity. Break them down into manageable chunks. Be very methodical and deliberate, and guide your child each step of the way. By having your guidance for the first experiment, your child will be ready for a little more independence on the next one.

Life Science

Within the area of life science, your child will be studying the characteristics of organisms (living things) as well as the role organisms play in a living system (habitat). Specifically, your child will be studying the adaptive characteristics of organisms and how organisms can survive only in environments that meet their needs. For example, a cactus has adapted to the harsh, dry conditions found in hot, arid climates by storing water. In addition, the cactus has sharp needles that help defend it against other organisms seeking the water stored within the cactus.

Your child will also be studying the difference between inherited and learned traits. Inherited traits have a genetic component, such as whether your hair is straight, wavy, or curly; the shape of your hands; the sound of your voice; the color of your eyes; or the length of your legs. Learned traits include such things as being able to read, how to speak a language, or what type of music you enjoy. There are some traits that have both an inherited and a learned aspect, such as personality. There is a genetic predisposition toward a certain personality, but personality is also shaped by learned characteristics. For example, a person may be genetically predisposed to having a quick temper, but there is a learned component in how to manage (or not manage) that temper.

The following table describes some skills related to life science, where children can run into problems, and what you can do to help them along.

Life Science Skills	Having Trouble?	Quick Tips
Identifies adapted characteristics of plants and animals.	Can't identify characteristics that plants and animals develop over time.	Compare the eating habits of an animal raised indoors to the same animal that lives in the wild. For example, housecats eat cat food, whereas wild cats eat mice, snakes, and birds. Domestic dogs eat dog food, while wild dogs eat birds, chickens, and squirrels.
Classifies characteristics as inherited or learned.	Mixes up characteristics that are inherited or learned.	It's all about me! Try helping your child identify things about himself that are inherited (hair color) and those that are learned (riding a bicycle).

Life Science Activities

1 Adaptive Concentration

TIME: 10–15 minutes

MATERIALS
12 index cards
crayons or markers

Write the following on six of the index cards: "a bear's thick fur"; "a cow's flat teeth"; "a lion's sharp teeth"; "a duck's webbed feet"; "a rabbit's long ears"; and "a chameleon's ability to change color." On the other six cards, write: "tolerate cold conditions"; "grind grass"; "tear meat"; "swim"; "hear faint sounds"; and "blend into the surroundings."

Learning occurs when: you shuffle the cards and placed them face-down in a 4 × 3 grid. Your child will pick two cards. A match is a card that has an adaptive characteristic (such as "a bear's thick fur") and a card that explains how a characteristic helps the animal survive ("tolerate cold conditions"). If the cards match, your child gets to keep the cards and take another turn. This continues until your child does not make a match. When no match is made, the cards are placed back into their original positions, facedown, and it's the next player's turn. When all the matches have been made, each player will count his cards. The person with the most cards wins.

Variations: Have your child research adaptive characteristics to make his own set of cards. You can then play the game together, using the cards your child has made.

- ✋ Playing the game, moving the cards, and making matches will help kinesthetic learners understand this concept.
- 👁 Visual learners will enjoy making their own sets of cards.
- 👂 Auditory learners may need to do some self-talk to see if the adaptive characteristic matches how it helps the organism survive.

Mastery occurs when: your child can match the adaptive characteristic to how it helps the organism survive.

You may want to help your child a little more if: he is having trouble making the matches. Separate the cards into two piles: characteristics and actions. Then ask this generic, fill-in-the-blank question to see if the cards match: does (this characteristic card) help the animal (this action card)? For example, if your child picked a "swim" and "a lion's sharp teeth," ask, "Does a lion's sharp teeth help it to swim?" If the answer is yes, you have a match. If the answer is no, there is no match.

2 Supportive Environments

On six of the cards, write the following environments: "a forest," "an ocean," "a lake," "a swamp," "the Arctic," and "a desert." On the other six cards, write the following animals: "deer," "whale," "catfish," "alligator," "penguin," and "camel."

TIME: 20–30 minutes

MATERIALS

12 index cards

crayons or markers

Learning occurs when: your child plays a game of Concentration and matches the environment to the animal it is most likely to support. Shuffle the cards and place them facedown in a 4 × 3 grid. The first player picks two cards, trying to match the animal with the environment that is most supportive for that animal. If a match is made, the player keeps the cards and takes another turn. This continues until no match is made. Then it's the other player's turn. The person who has the most cards after all the matches have been made is the winner.

Variations: Once your child has done this activity and readily knows which animal matches what environment, use a stopwatch to time your child to see how quickly she can make the matches.

✋ Kinesthetic learners will enjoy flipping the cards and making the matches.

👁 Visual learners may want to help you create the cards and may want to make a list of the animals and their environments.

👂 Auditory learners may need to think aloud as they are matching up the cards.

Mastery occurs when: your child can match each animal to its environment.

You may want to help your child a little more if: she is having trouble making the matches. Play the game faceup and see if your child can simply match each animal with its environment. Once she is comfortable with that, play the game as outlined earlier.

3 Design a Habitat

TIME: 30–45 minutes

MATERIALS
- paper
- pencils
- shoebox
- basic craft supplies, such as a large sheet of construction paper, non-toxic glue, rounded-edge scissors, etc.

Learning occurs when: your child creates a diorama of a habitat suitable for an animal of his choice. Talk to your child about the fact that a suitable habitat must meet the needs of the organism living there. The habitat must provide five things: food, water, air, space, and shelter. Have your child write the five things the habitat must have to support his animal on a piece of paper. To make the diorama, your child should turn the shoebox on its side and create a scene in the box using the craft supplies you have available. Your child can cross the five things off the list as he adds them to the diorama.

Variations: Your child can draw a picture or make a poster of a suitable habitat for his animal.

✋ Creating a habitat will help kinesthetic learners think about how the habitat meets the needs of the animal.

👁 Seeing the habitat set up in the diorama will help visual learners understand how the habitat supports the animal.

👂 Discuss with your auditory learner how his habitat meets the needs of the animal.

Mastery occurs when: your child creates a diorama of a habitat that meets the five needs of his animal and can explain how the habitat meets the animal's needs.

You may want to help your child a little more if: he did not meet all five needs of the animal. Ask your child to show you where the animal will get food. If the animal eats insects, your child needs to include insects in the diorama. Ask him to show you where the animal will find shelter. Continue asking questions until all the animal's needs are met.

4 | Starring Roles

Write the following organisms on the index cards: "grass," "bush," "tree," "flower," "deer," "moose," "rabbit," "squirrel," "wolf," "hawk," "bear," and "snake." On the three paper plates, write the following: "producer," "herbivore," and "carnivore."

Learning occurs when: your child categorizes organisms according to their role in an ecosystem. There are two main types of organisms: producers and consumers. Producers create their own food. Plants are producers, because they make their own food through the process of photosynthesis. Consumers rely on other organisms as food sources. Two types of consumers are herbivores (plant eaters) and carnivores (animal eaters.) Your child should categorize each organism according to whether it is a producer, an herbivore, or a carnivore. Shuffle the organism cards and place them facedown. Set out the three plates. Your child should flip

TIME: 20–30 minutes

MATERIALS
- 12 index cards
- 3 paper plates
- crayons or markers

over a card, decide in which category the organism on the card belongs, and place the card on the correct plate. Continue until there are no cards left. Your child earns one point for each correct answer. The grass, bush, tree, and flower cards should be on the producer plate; the deer, moose, rabbit, and squirrel cards should be on the herbivore plate; and the wolf, hawk, bear, and snake cards should be on the carnivore plate.

To earn extra points, ask your child what would happen if a drought occurred. (There would be fewer producers.) What would then happen to the herbivores? (There would not be enough food, so some of the herbivores would die.) What would then happen to the carnivores? (There would not be enough food for the carnivores, so some of them would also die.) Your child should understand that the herbivores rely on the producers for food, and that the carnivores rely mostly on herbivores for food. When one of the groups is adversely affected, all the groups are adversely affected.

Variations: If your child likes to race the clock, use a stopwatch to time her as she completes this activity.

- Kinesthetic learners will learn by flipping the cards and placing them on the correct plates.
- Visual learners may enjoy helping you make the cards.
- Have auditory learners explain their thinking as they complete the activity.

Mastery occurs when: your child can correctly categorize the organisms and understands the interdependence among them.

You may want to help your child a little more if: she is having trouble categorizing an organism. Ask your child what that organism eats. If it does not eat (which is an answer your child will give for the producers), it makes its own food, so it must be a producer. If it eats grass and leaves, it is an herbivore. If it eats other animals, it is a carnivore. Once you feel your child understands the categories, try the game again.

5 | Classified Animals

On the index cards, write "deer," "mouse," "dog," "cat," "fox," "bird," "snake," "turtle," "chicken," and "alligator." On one paper plate write "mammal." On the other paper plate write "lays eggs." On the second set of index cards, write "bat," "mosquito," "parrot," "bee," "butterfly," "dolphin," "octopus," "eel," "seahorse," and "jellyfish." On one paper plate write "fly" and on the other write "swim."

TIME: 30–45 minutes

MATERIALS
20 index cards
4 paper plates
crayons or markers

Learning occurs when: your child classifies a stack of animal cards into groups. Shuffle the first set of index cards and place them in a stack facedown. Set out the first two paper plates. Have your child go through the cards and put each of them on the correct paper plate. When your child is done, have him classify the second set of index cards.

Variations: Decide on one characteristic and pull only the animal cards that share that characteristic. See if your child can tell what they all have in common. For example, you may pull all the animal cards for animals with four legs, or animals with no legs, animals that have scales, or animals that have fur.

- ✋ Kinesthetic learners will learn from flipping the cards and placing them on the correct plates.
- 👁 Visual learners will enjoy helping you to create the cards.
- 👂 Have auditory learners discuss things they notice about each animal and explain why they are putting them in a category.

Mastery occurs when: your child can correctly classify all of the animal cards.

You may want to help your child a little more if: he is having trouble classifying. Start with a simple classification, such as pulling all the cards that have animals that live in the ocean. Have your child tell you what is the same about the animals. Continue, using very straightforward categories. Once your child can pull the cards for one category only, have him pull each card and decide in which of two categories the card belongs.

6 Trait Swats

TIME: 10–15 minutes

MATERIALS
- 10 index cards
- 2 paper plates
- crayons or markers
- clean fly swatter

On five of the index cards, write the following inherited traits: "eye color," "type of hair" (curly, wavy, or straight), "shape of face," "shoe size," and "height." On the other five index cards, write the following learned traits: "eating habits," "riding a bike," "speaking English," "reading," and "taste in food." On the paper plates write "Learned Trait" and "Inherited Trait."

Learning occurs when: your child plays a game distinguishing inherited traits from learned traits. Place the paper plates on a table. Shuffle the index cards and place them facedown. Draw a card and read it. Your child will then take the fly swatter and swat one of the paper plates, depending on whether the trait on the card is inherited or learned. For example, you draw the reading card and say, "Reading." Your child will swat the learned trait plate, because reading is something you learn. Your child scores one point for each correct swat. Continue until all the cards have been played.

Variations: Once your child can complete this activity with 100 percent accuracy, have her research inherited traits and learned traits to make her own set of cards.

☝ Kinesthetic learners will do well with this activity because of the action of swatting the plates.

👁 Visual learners may want to arrange the cards on the correct plates.

👂 Auditory learners may want to think aloud to determine what kind of trait is being called.

Mastery occurs when: your child can tell the difference between learned and inherited traits and can categorize these traits accordingly.

You may want to help your child a little more if: she is having difficulty categorizing the traits. Make sure your child understands the difference between learned traits and inherited traits.

7 | Trait Survey

Learning occurs when: your child plans and conducts a survey to determine how many people have certain inherited traits. Some interesting inherited traits include the ability to roll the tongue, whether the earlobes are attached at the bottom or hang down, and whether the index finger is longer or shorter than the ring finger. Have your child design questions about these three inherited traits and survey at least twenty people to see which traits they inherited. Your child should survey people he knows, such as classmates, friends, and family members. Once your child has conducted the survey, have him tabulate the results.

TIME: 45–60 minutes

MATERIALS
paper
pencils

Variations: Have your child research dominant (visible) and recessive (hidden) traits and then determine what dominant traits he has and what recessive traits he has.

👐 Kinesthetic learners will benefit from the interactive learning that comes from interviewing people for information.

👁 Visual learners would benefit from graphing the results.

👂 Have auditory learners present the results orally.

Mastery occurs when: your child designs and conducts a well-thought-out survey and communicates the results in an organized, clear fashion.

You may want to help your child a little more if: he is overwhelmed by this task. Break down the task into manageable parts. Have your child complete one part before moving on to the other part of the task.

Physical Science and Earth Science

In physical science, your child will be learning about position and motion. Specifically, she will investigate how position and motion can be changed by pushing and pulling. Your child has already experimented with this concept on the playground. For example, if you ask her how to make a swing go higher when someone is pushing it, she can probably tell you the person must push harder. The merry-go-round is another example of position and motion being changed by pushing and pulling.

Another concept your child will be studying in physical science is electricity and how the flow of electricity is controlled by opening and closing circuits. When a circuit is closed, electricity flows. An analogy of how this works is to think of a circular toy train track. When the track is closed, the train can go around the track easily. If there is an opening somewhere on the track, the train will stop at that open spot.

Finally, your child will be learning about matter. Matter is anything that takes up space and has mass. Basically, everything is made of matter. Your child will be examining how matter can be changed by adding or reducing heat. When something is heated, the molecules of the substance move more quickly, which makes the material expand. There are many examples of this in real life. For example, sidewalks are made with cracks in between so that the sidewalk can expand a little in the summer. If the spaces were not there, the sidewalk would still expand, but because there is no room in which it can expand, the sidewalk would buckle and crack. When most substances are cooled, the molecules move more slowly and the substance contracts slightly. But there is a glaring exception to the rule of things contracting as they get cold: frozen water. When water is frozen, it expands slightly. You can show this by completely filling a plastic bottle with water, capping it tightly, and putting it in the freezer. When the water freezes, it will expand. Because there is no room for the water to expand, the plastic bottle might crack to make room for the expanding water.

Your child will also be studying the phases of matter: solid, liquid, and gas. The phases of matter can all be demonstrated using water as an example:

- Solid: ice

- Liquid: water

- Gas: steam

Earth science will be a relatively small portion of the fourth grade year. Your child will look at weathering, erosion, sediment, and fossils. Weathering is the process of rock being worn down by water, wind, or some other means. Weathered rock particles are a major component of soil. Erosion is the process of weathered rock particles being carried away by wind, water, or some other means. Sedimentation is the tendency of dense material to settle at the bottom. For example, as particles are being carried away by erosion, the larger particles will settle at the bottom, with the smallest particles settling at the top. Fossils are the remains of former living things that are found in the rocks in the earth's crust. Fossils can include teeth, bones, impressions, casts, and so on.

The following table describes some skills related to physical science, where children can run into problems, and what you can do to help them along.

Physical Science Skills	Having Problems?	Quick Tips
Knows what an electrical circuit is.	Doesn't understand what an electrical circuit is or why it is necessary.	Blow air (or water) through a straw. The flow through the straw is analogous to an open circuit. Next put a couple drops of water in the straw, then bend it into a circle, sticking one end inside the other. This is analogous to a closed circuit.
Knows the phases of matter.	Cannot identify the three different forms of matter.	The forms of matter that water can take are the clearest examples you can find. You can find all three forms in the kitchen and you can find liquid and steam in the bathroom. Talk about these forms of matter in daily life until your child understands them.

Physical Science Activities

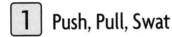 Push, Pull, Swat

TIME: 15–20 minutes

MATERIALS
- 10 index cards
- 2 paper plates
- crayons or markers
- clean fly swatter

On five of the index cards, write the following five actions that most likely require pushing: "moving a wheelbarrow," "moving a shopping cart," "closing the car door from outside the car," "moving a stroller," and "moving a vacuum cleaner." On the other five index cards, write the following five actions that most likely require pulling: "moving a wagon," "playing a game of tug-of-war," "closing a car door from inside the car," "closing the curtains," and "raising a flag up a flagpole." On the paper plates, write "push" and "pull."

Learning occurs when: your child plays a game to determine if an object is moved by pushing or pulling. Shuffle the index cards and place them facedown. Draw a card and read it to your child. He will then swat the correct plate with the fly swatter. For example, you draw the card "moving a vacuum cleaner" and read it aloud. Your child will swat the "push" plate, because that action is usually accomplished by pushing. For some of the actions, he may argue that the object can be moved by the opposite force. This is true, but have him tell you which force is more commonly used.

Variations: Have your child think of actions to add to the bunch. Reverse roles, have your child read the cards to you, and you determine the force involved.

- Kinesthetic learners will do well with this activity because of the action of swatting the plates.

- Visual learners may want to arrange the cards on the correct plates.

- Auditory learners may want to think aloud to determine what kind of force is used.

Mastery occurs when: your child understands the difference between pushing and pulling, and can determine if an object is moved by pushing or pulling.

You may want to help your child a little more if: he is having trouble distinguishing between the two actions. Explain that pushing is moving an object away from your body. Pulling is moving an object toward your body. Have your child act out the action and see if the object is being moved away from or toward his body.

2 | Closed or Open Circuit?

TIME: 20–30 minutes

MATERIALS

- 4 × 6-inch index card
- hole punch
- pencils
- aluminum foil
- rounded-edge scissors
- masking tape
- paper
- circuit tester (available at hardware or home improvement stores)

Learning occurs when: your child uses a circuit tester to determine if a circuit is closed or open. Have your child use the hole punch to punch four holes across the top of the index card. Then have her punch four holes across the bottom of the index card. Label the top holes "A," "B," "C," and "D." Label the bottom holes "1," "2," "3," and "4." It should look something like this:

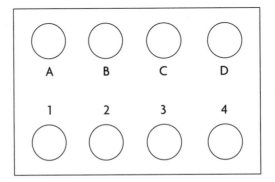

Turn the card over. Your child should cut narrow strips of aluminum foil to connect each letter hole to one number hole. Make sure each strip is long enough to reach from hole to hole and that the aluminum foil covers the openings of the two holes completely. Be very careful that the strip does not touch any other hole. Secure the aluminum foil strips with masking tape. Completely cover the strip with the tape, being very careful to not tape over any other hole. The masking tape should act as a barrier so that none of the strips of foil touch each other. After the card is finished, turn it over. On the paper, draw a table similar to the one on page 159:

Your child will test each letter with each number to see if the circuit is open or closed. The circuit tester has two ends. Have your child put one end on the foil in the letter A hole and the

Letter	Number	Closed	Open

other end on the foil in the number 1 hole. If the circuit is closed, the circuit tester will light up. If the circuit is open, the circuit tester will remain unlit. Your child should write A in the first column and 1 in the second column, and will mark a checkmark under "Closed" or "Open," depending on her findings. After testing A1, test A2. Then do A3 and A4. After A has been tested with each number, move on to B. Continue testing all the letters with all the numbers.

Variations: Have your child make circuit tester cards for different subjects, for example, math problems and their answers, vocabulary words and their definitions, or characters and their stories. The circuit is closed when your child solves the problem or matches the vocabulary word with the definition.

✋ Kinesthetic learners will enjoy working with the circuit tester.

👁 Visual learners will learn from seeing how the circuit is completed.

👂 Discuss what is happening with your auditory learner as you are making the circuit tester.

Mastery occurs when: your child understands how the circuit tester works and can tell the difference between an open circuit and a closed circuit.

You may want to help your child a little more if: she is not understanding the difference between an open circuit and a closed circuit. Use the train track analogy as detailed in the beginning of this section.

3 | Conductor or Insulator?

TIME: 10–15 minutes

MATERIALS
▓ several small items made of metal (conductors)
▓ several small items made of wood, rubber, or plastic (insulators)
▓ circuit tester (available at hardware or home improvement stores)
▓ paper
▓ pencils

Learning occurs when: your child uses the circuit tester to determine if an item is a conductor or an insulator. Conductors are things through which electricity can flow, while insulators are things through which electricity cannot flow. Some conductors you can find around the house include coins, paper clips, metal spoons, safety pins, and screws. Some insulators you can find around the house include erasers, wooden spoons, plastic toys, plastic cups, and rubber bands. Your child will test each object by putting both ends of the circuit tester on the item to be tested. If the tester lights up, the object is a conductor. If the tester does not light up, the object is an insulator. Be careful, because objects can be made of more than one type of material. For example, a screwdriver has a shaft that is a conductor but a handle that is an insulator. Try to pick objects made of one type of material. Have your child keep track of the results by making a three-column table on a piece of paper. Label the first column "Object," the second column "Conductor," and the third column "Insulator." Have your child write the name of the object in the first column and put an "X" in the column that describes the object as either a conductor or an insulator.

Variations: Have your child find a certain number of conductors in a certain area. For example, find ten conductors in the kitchen. Do the same thing for insulators.

✋ Kinesthetic learners will enjoy working with the circuit tester.

👁 Visual learners will benefit from keeping track of their results in a tabular format.

👂 Discuss with your auditory learner what's going on as he tests each object.

Mastery occurs when: your child understands the difference between a conductor and an insulator and can predict before testing whether an item will be a conductor or an insulator.

You may want to help your child a little more if: he is having trouble distinguishing conductors from insulators. Make sure your child understands what each term means. Also, make sure he is using the circuit tester correctly. Do a few with your child so he can learn by watching you.

4 | Invisible Forces

Learning occurs when: you demonstrate for your child what happens when heated air cools. Pour two cups of very hot water into the milk jug through the funnel. Allow this to sit uncapped for three minutes. Quickly pour out the water and replace the cap tightly. Observe what happens as the air inside cools. It is almost as if an invisible hand is crushing the milk jug. Explain to your child that pouring the hot water into the jug and allowing it to sit for a few minutes heated the air inside the jug. As the air heated it expanded, and some escaped out of the top of the jug. After you poured the water out, the heat source was gone. By quickly capping the jug, no air could come into or out of the jug. As the air inside the jug cooled, it contracted, or got smaller. The air contracting inside the jug combined with the air pressure outside the jug, and as a result the jug started to collapse.

TIME: 10–15 minutes

MATERIALS
- clean, clear plastic, empty $1/2$ or gallon milk jug with cap
- measuring cup
- funnel
- hot water

Variations: You could use a plastic water bottle to demonstrate the same principle.

✋ Your kinesthetic learner will probably beg you to let her do this activity on her own; just make sure you help her handle the hot water safely.

👁 Seeing the results will help visual learners understand the science behind the demonstration.

👂 Discussing what happened and why will help auditory learners understand the science more clearly.

Mastery occurs when: your child understands what happened to the milk jug and why.

You may want to help your child a little more if: she does not understand the point of the demonstration. She may think this is a neat magic trick, but the point is that heat makes things expand and cooling makes things contract. Reinforce with other examples after the demonstration.

5 Hot Bubbles

TIME: 30 minutes

MATERIALS
▪ ⅓ cup of dish soap
▪ 1 cup of water
▪ 1 teaspoon of sugar
▪ container for bubble solution
▪ bubble blowers

Learning occurs when: your child explores how heat affects the formation and activity of bubbles. This experiment needs to be completed on a cold day. Mix the dish soap, water, and sugar together. Put the solution in a container and heat it in the microwave for a few seconds until it is warm. Immediately take the warm solution outside and blow bubbles. What observations does your child make about the bubbles created on a cold day, using warmed solution? Cold air is heavier than warm air. The heavier cold air sinks to the ground, while warmer air rises. By using warm solution and a warm breath to create the bubbles on a cold day, the warm bubbles rise very quickly into the air.

Variations: After making the solution, put half of it in the refrigerator. After the solution has cooled, warm the other half of the solution in the microwave. Take both solutions outside and blow bubbles. Do the bubbles made with the warm solution behave differently than the bubbles made with the cold solution? Discuss any observations with your child.

🖐 Experimenting with the warmed solution will help kinesthetic learners understand how heat affects the bubbles.

👁 Visual learners will benefit from seeing how quickly the warm bubbles rise.

👂 Auditory learners will benefit from discussing what happened.

Mastery occurs when: your child understands the effect of heat on the bubbles.

You may want to help your child a little more if: he does not see the warm bubbles rising quickly. Try the variation so your child can directly compare warm bubbles with cold bubbles.

6 | Measuring Erosion

Make a four-column table on the piece of paper. Label the first column "Date," the second column "Length," the third column "Width," and the fourth column "Height."

Learning occurs when: your child measures the effect of erosion on a mound of soil. In an area of your yard that will remain undisturbed, build a mound of soil about 50 centimeters high. Help

Time: 10 minutes each day during a week

Materials
- paper
- pencils
- an undisturbed area in the yard or a window box
- yardstick or tape measure
- soil

your child measure the length, width, and height of the mountain of soil. Note the date and the measurements on the table. These are the baseline measurements. One week later, take new measurements. Be sure to measure the length and width the same way each time. Note the date and new measurements on the table. Continue for twelve weeks. At the end of that time, discuss the findings with your child. What happened to the length? What about the width? What happened to the height? Why?

Variations: Have your child take pictures of the soil mountain at weekly intervals, in addition to measuring. Make a book about this experiment, complete with the pictures and measurements week by week.

- Kinesthetic learners will enjoy measuring and watching what happens to the soil mountain.
- Visual learners will probably enjoy the variation of this activity.
- Auditory learners will benefit from the discussion at the end of the experiment.

Mastery occurs when: your child accurately measures the soil mountain, notes the measurements, and understands the concept of erosion and its effect.

You may want to help your child a little more if: she is having difficulty with this activity. Make sure she understands how to measure accurately. Do it with your child, guiding her to ensure accuracy. Discuss changes with your child to help her to better understand what is happening.

7 | Sedimentation in a Jar

Learning occurs when: your child observes sedimentation in a jar. Have him add some gravel, sand, mud, silt, and clay to a large, wide-mouth jar. Add water to the contents, put a lid on the jar, and shake well. Have your child write down what he has done so far. Ask your child to make a prediction about what will happen if the jar is left alone for several days. Let the jar stand undisturbed for several days. After that time, ask your child to write down what he observed. After he has written down his observations, discuss them with him. Sedimentation is the tendency for particles with the most mass to settle at the bottom. The particles in the jar should have settled in layers so that the largest particles are on the bottom and the smallest particles are on the top. How can this experiment relate to erosion into rivers or other bodies of water?

TIME: 30 minutes the first day, 15 minutes on the follow-up day

MATERIALS
- large, wide-mouth glass jar
- gravel
- sand
- mud
- silt (from a garden store or outside)
- clay (from a garden store or outside)
- water
- paper

Variations: Gather some craft items such as glitter, small beads, or buttons. Predict how sedimentation would affect these items. What would settle at the bottom? What would be the next layer, and so forth? Conduct the experiment and see if the results match your prediction.

- ✋ Kinesthetic learners will enjoy setting up and conducting this experiment.
- 👁 Visual learners will receive reinforcement by seeing how the layers form.
- 👂 Auditory learners will receive reinforcement by discussing their observations.

Mastery occurs when: your child understands sedimentation and how particles layer according to mass.

You may want to help your child a little more if: he does not understand sedimentation. Ask your child to notice what is on the bottom of the jar. Why does he think that settled to the bottom? Your child may say something like, "It is the heaviest." That is correct, but scientists would say it has the most mass. Have your child look at the top layer. Why did that settle at the top? Your child may say, "It is the lightest." That is almost correct. The particles that settle to the top have the most surface area combined with the least mass. Explain to him that two substances that have the same mass (weight), the one with the most surface area (the bigger one) will settle at the top.

8 Making Fossils

Time: 40–50 minutes

MATERIALS
- ¹/₂ cup salt
- 1 cup flour
- ¹/₂ cup cold brewed coffee
- 1 cup used coffee grounds
- waxed paper
- items to imprint into the "stone" dough

Learning occurs when: your child creates imitation fossils. Fossils are the remains of once living things found in the rocks of the earth's crust. Fossils can include teeth, bones, shells, or even a rock that includes an impression of another fossil. Scientists make casts or molds that take the shape of a fossilized item. Make "stone" dough with your child by stirring together the salt, flour, brewed coffee, and coffee grounds. Knead the dough on waxed paper until smooth. Gather items to use as fossils. These can include twigs, stiff leaves, seashells, and so on. Pull off enough stone dough to make an imprint with one of the items. Roll the dough into a ball and flatten. Press an object into the dough to make a fossil imprint. Continue pulling the stone dough, rolling, flattening, and pressing for each of the other items. Let the impressions dry overnight and remove the item that made the impression, and your child will have imitation fossils.

Variations: Instead of making the dough, your child can make fossils using plaster of paris. Make a bowl with a sheet of aluminum foil. Fill the aluminum-foil bowl with plaster of paris and press items into it. Wait twenty to thirty minutes. Carefully remove the items and the aluminum foil.

- Creating their own fossils will help kinesthetic learners better understand this concept.
- Visual learners will better understand fossils by seeing their creation.
- Auditory learners may need to discuss their observations.

Mastery occurs when: your child understands what a fossil is.

You may want to help your child a little more if: she is having trouble connecting this activity to real fossils. A fossil is often created when a living thing dies. An impression of that living thing sometimes is made in the mud. As layers are created on top of the mud through erosion and other processes, the mud is compressed and becomes rock over time. The impression, which was in the mud, is now a part of the rock.

Environmental Learning

Every time you step into the kitchen you have the opportunity to reinforce fourth grade science concepts. Cooking is a scientific process, and certain steps must be taken before other steps. Cooking often changes the form of matter that your ingredients start out in. It also can be used to give examples of inherited traits (allergies, the need to eat), learned traits (how to cook), and adaptive traits (eating something new). As always, applying what your child learns in school to the real world drives home the new concepts and skills.

End of Fourth Grade Science Checklist

Students who are working at the standard level at the end of fourth grade:

____ Have begun to use scientific methods

____ Can identify pushing and pulling as a means to change the position of an object

____ Understand closed and open electric circuits

____ Know how matter is changed by adding or reducing heat

____ Can identify adaptive characteristics in organisms

____ Know that the needs of organisms must be met by their environment

____ Can classify organisms and know the roles of organisms in living systems

____ Can distinguish between inherited and learned traits

____ Can identify the effects of weathering, erosion, and sedimentation

Fourth Grade Social Studies

9

In fourth grade social studies, your child will continue to learn about the geography of the United States, particularly the five regions of the country: the Northeast, the Southeast, the Midwest, the Southwest and the West. Your child will be expected to know the similarities and differences of each region and the reasons the states were grouped together into regions.

Your child will also be required to identify where each state is on a map and name its capital, and to know the major cities in the United States. Your child will also focus on state and local governing bodies and civic participation.

Beginning of Fourth Grade Social Studies Checklist

Students who are working on the standard level at the beginning of fourth grade:

____ Can create symbols for real-life objects

____ Can identify cardinal directions on a map

____ Can identify intermediate directions on a map

____ Can identify the equator and the prime meridian

____ Can identify the four hemispheres of the earth

____ Can identify basic landforms

____ Understand the law of supply and demand

____ Can set a financial goal and make a plan to accomplish the goal

---

Geography

Because your child will focus mainly on the five regions of the United States, it would be a good idea to see what states are considered to be

Northeast	Southeast	Midwest	Southwest	West
Connecticut	Alabama	Illinois	Arizona	Alaska
Delaware	Arkansas	Indiana	New Mexico	California
Maine	Florida	Iowa	Oklahoma	Colorado
Maryland	Georgia	Kansas	Texas	Hawaii
Massachusetts	Kentucky	Michigan		Idaho
New Hampshire	Louisiana	Minnesota		Montana
New Jersey	Mississippi	Missouri		Nevada
New York	North Carolina	Nebraska		Oregon
Pennsylvania	South Carolina	North Dakota		Utah
Rhode Island	Tennessee	Ohio		Washington
Vermont	Virginia	South Dakota		Wyoming
	West Virginia	Wisconsin		

in each region. The table on this page will help you identify the states in each region.

Your child will also be learning about the types of landforms in each region, such as bays, bluffs, canyons, cliffs, coasts, deserts, gulfs, harbors, hills, islands, lakes, and mountains. (For a complete listing of landforms and their definitions, go to www.knowledgeessentials.com.)

The table on page 171 describes some skills related to geography, where children can run into problems, and what you can do to help them along.

Geography Skills	Having Problems?	Quick Tips
Points out regions of the United States on a map.	Confuses regions of the United States.	Try drawing a compass rose over a U.S. map. The point where the regions intersect is the "heartland," and the areas in each quadrant relate generally to the cardinal directions.
Understands the many kinds of maps.	Can't get past the idea that maps do more than get you from here to there.	Start with your state map and talk about what that map tells you (the shape of your state). Get a blank state map (available at www .knowledgeessentials.com) and ask your child to draw in symbols that he makes up to represent things that he knows about your state (such as an X for every place a family member lives). Once your child understands the concept from his own map, try reading a population map together.

Geography Activities

1 Region Map

Learning happens when: your child labels all of the states on the outline map of the United States. Next, ask him to use the colored pencils to define each region of the United States by using a different color. Make a map key to identify which color stands for which region.

Variations: You could also have your child label the state capital or one of the largest or most important cities in the region.

TIME: 25 minutes

MATERIALS
- outline map of the United States (you can find one at www .knowledgeessentials.com)
- region chart from page 170
- 5 pencils of different colors

✋ Instead of coloring, your kinesthetic learner could use different materials to cover each region. This material could be something with a distinctive texture, such as cotton or velvet, so that your child would be able to feel the difference as well as see it on the map. You could also have him trace the outline of each region with his finger.

👁 Visual learners will benefit from being able to see the colored regions and their shapes on the map.

👂 Auditory learners can say the name of the region and then recite each of the states in each region.

Mastery occurs when: your child can identify the five regions of the United States.

You might want to help your child a little more if: he can't identify the regions of the United States. Try tracing around each region using a colored pencil and then having him color the region.

2 | Fifty Nifty

TIME: 20–30 minutes

MATERIALS
▪ The song "Fifty Nifty" (you can find a link to the lyrics at www .knowledgeessentials.com)

Learning happens when: your child listens to and sings along with the song. As the song progresses, you should increase the speed at which you and your child sing. Your child should repeat this several times.

Variations: your child could have a map of the United States and point to each state as she sings its name.

✋ Kinesthetic learners should do the variation of the activity with the map of the United States in front of them. It would be good for them to also touch the state as the name of the state is being sung.

👁 Visual learners would also benefit from doing the variation.

👂 Auditory learners will be fine with the activity as it is originally described.

Mastery occurs when: your child can say or sing the names of the fifty states.

You might want to help your child a little more if: she is having a hard time remembering the names of all the states. Let your child look at the words of the song as she listens and sings along. Gradually take away the list.

3 | State Capital Rap

Learning happens when: your child creates a rap with the names of the states and their capitals. He can use drums or other musical instruments to add a beat to his rap. Rapping to learn is more about the beat than original words. Try rapping the states in alphabetical order, followed by the capitals. You can rap the capital while your child responds by rapping the state or vice versa. Rap the regions, each to a different beat. There are many ways you can rap states and capitals and all of them help your child memorize the names.

Variations: if your child doesn't feel comfortable with a rap, he could write a regular song or a poem.

✋ Kinesthetic learners will enjoy using drums to play along as they perform.

👁 Visual learners might want to make signs with each state's outline and capital to use as visual aids.

TIME: 20–30 minutes

MATERIALS
▫ list of the states with their capitals (see the "State Capitals" table on page 174)
▫ drums (or anything that makes a beat)

State Capitals

State	Capital	State	Capital
Alabama	Montgomery	Montana	Helena
Alaska	Juneau	Nebraska	Lincoln
Arizona	Phoenix	Nevada	Carson City
Arkansas	Little Rock	New Hampshire	Concord
California	Sacramento	New Jersey	Trenton
Colorado	Denver	New Mexico	Santa Fe
Connecticut	Hartford	New York	Albany
Delaware	Dover	North Carolina	Raleigh
Florida	Tallahassee	North Dakota	Bismarck
Georgia	Atlanta	Ohio	Columbus
Hawaii	Honolulu	Oklahoma	Oklahoma City
Idaho	Boise	Oregon	Salem
Illinois	Springfield	Pennsylvania	Harrisburg
Indiana	Indianapolis	Rhode Island	Providence
Iowa	Des Moines	South Carolina	Columbia
Kansas	Topeka	South Dakota	Pierre
Kentucky	Frankfort	Tennessee	Nashville
Louisiana	Baton Rouge	Texas	Austin
Maine	Augusta	Utah	Salt Lake City
Maryland	Annapolis	Vermont	Montpelier
Massachusetts	Boston	Virginia	Richmond
Michigan	Lansing	Washington	Olympia
Minnesota	St. Paul	West Virginia	Charleston
Mississippi	Jackson	Wisconsin	Madison
Missouri	Jefferson City	Wyoming	Cheyenne

🦻 Auditory learners will do well with the chanting and rhyming in this activity.

Mastery occurs when: your child can remember each state and its capital.

You might want to help your child a little more if: he can't remember all of the capitals of the states. Try letting your child use a copy of the lyrics until he can perform the rap without looking at them.

4 Region Poems

Learning happens when: you and your child discuss the characteristics of the region of the United States that you live in. Brainstorm with her about what might go in a poem about your region, then ask your child to write a poem about it. The poem could include stanzas about major landforms, climate, natural resources, wildlife, industries, and major cities.

Variations: Write poems about other regions of the United States.

🖐 Kinesthetic learners could look through magazines and find pictures to illustrate each stanza.

👁 Visual learners would also benefit from using illustrations to go with each stanza of the poem.

🦻 Auditory learners should read the poem aloud.

Mastery occurs when: your child can remember information about your region.

You might want to help your child a little more if: she can't remember any information about the region after writing the poem. Try having her recite or sing the poem a few times to help her remember. Illustrating the poem should also help her retain the information.

TIME: 30 minutes

MATERIALS
- paper
- pencils
- information about your region of the United States

5 | Region Cluster

Learning happens when: your child chooses a region of the United States and finds information about it at the library or on the Internet. Ask your child to organize the information he has learned onto a cluster map like this one:

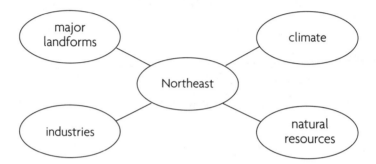

The name of the region should go in the center oval. Then draw four ovals around the center oval. Label these ovals: "major landforms," "climate," "natural resources," and "industries." Each oval should be connected to the center oval by a line. Information about each topic in the four ovals should be written on the lines. When your child has completed the cluster map, he should use it to give an oral report about the region.

Variations: Instead of creating a cluster map, your child could use an outline to organize the information.

✋ Kinesthetic learners might want to do the cluster map on the computer.

👁 The activity is suitable for visual learners because they are producing a visual aid for the information.

👂 Auditory learners will do fine with the activity the way it is written because they will give an oral report about the region.

Mastery occurs when: your child can organize the information in a cluster map and give a short report about the region.

You might want to help your child a little more if: he has trouble making the cluster map or can't give an oral report about the region. Try walking your child through the process of finding and organizing the information into categories. Before he gives the presentation, help him to write down what he is going to say about each topic.

6 | Secret Regions

Learning happens when: your child picks a region and creates a secret box. Give your child these topics to investigate about the region she has chosen: major landforms, climate, natural resources, wildlife, plants, and major cities. Have your child write the topics on separate index cards and choose some type of object to represent each topic (for example, Texas: oil; southwest: desert). Your child should then attach the appropriate index card to each object and put in the box. If some objects are too large, see if you can find a picture of the object to put in the box instead. When all of the objects have been placed in the box, put the lid on and then decorate the box. Ask another family member or a friend to use the object clues to try to guess what region of the United States the object represents.

Variations: You could make the object clues yourself and have your child figure out what the region is.

 The activity is fine as it is for kinesthetic learners because they are moving around and touching the objects to use as clues.

The activity is also fine for visual learners, as the objects are all visual clues.

TIME: 30 minutes

MATERIALS
- shoe box
- large sheet of construction paper
- crayons or markers
- index cards
- various items to represent the region

👂 Auditory learners should give a short oral report about how each object represents the region.

Mastery occurs when: your child can choose the objects that represent the characteristics of a particular region.

You might want to help your child a little more if: she can't figure out what to use to represent each topic. Try giving some hints for each topic.

7 | Where Do the Most People Live?

TIME: 15 minutes

MATERIALS
population map of the United States (you can find one at www .knowledgeessentials.com)

Learning happens when: your child looks at a population map of the United States. Ask him questions about the map. For example, what part of the United States has the largest population? Another question might be, why do you think this area has such a high population compared to this area?

Variations: Instead of asking him questions about the map, put your child in charge and let him ask you the questions. Try the same activity with a climate or a vegetation map (available at www.knowledgeessentials.com).

✋ Your kinesthetic learner might want to first complete the population map as a puzzle.

👁 This activity will work well for visual learners the way it is written because the map is a visual aid.

👂 Auditory learners will also do fine with the activity as it is written because all of the questions are asked orally.

Mastery occurs when: your child can give accurate answers to the questions about the population map.

You might want to help your child a little more if: he can't answer the questions about the map. Try focusing your questions on the region in which you live and then expand to the other regions.

8 Topographic Map

Learning happens when: your child examines the topographic map. She will be able to touch and feel the differences in height and size of the various landforms in the United States. Have your child create a chart like the one on page 180 and fill in the specific name of each landform on the map and any questions she might have about it (you can find this and other helpful charts at www.knowledgeessentials.com).

TIME: 30–40 minutes

MATERIALS
- topographic map of the United States
- pencils
- paper

Variations: You could group the landforms into separate types, such as those that have water and those that don't. You could already have questions on the chart that you want your child to answer. You could also add a column for answering the questions.

- This activity is naturally appealing to the kinesthetic learner. The topographic map allows her to touch and feel the size and shape of the various landforms.

- This activity is also appealing to visual learners because they can see the differences between the various landforms.

- Auditory learners might want to pretend that they are in an airplane flying over the United States and describe the landforms they are seeing.

Mastery occurs when: your child can see the differences in the size and shape of the landforms and can answer questions about them.

Type of Landform	Specific Name of Landform	Questions?
Mountain ranges	The Rocky Mountains	Which mountain range in the United States has the highest elevation?
Oceans		
Plains		
Rivers		
Islands		
Canyons		
Deserts		
Peninsulas		
Harbors		

You might want to help your child a little more if: she cannot answer your questions about the landforms. You might try limiting your question to one type of landform at a time.

Government

Who's in charge of our city and state? Who makes the laws? How are local and city governments set up? These are some of the things your child will learn in fourth grade. To help support what he or she is learning, focus on teaching your child about your town's government. This will provide a basis for understanding the municipal level of government.

Government Activities

1 What's Your Job?

Learning happens when: your child prepares questions to ask a local government official. Some sample questions include:

TIME: 20–30 minutes

MATERIALS
- tape recorder
- paper
- pencils

- What is your official job title?

- What are some of the responsibilities of your job?

- Do you mainly work alone or with a group?

- Describe a typical day for you on the job.

When your child has made a list of questions, talk to someone from your local government about setting up an interview. Have your child practice his interview skills on you or another adult, and use a tape recorder to tape the practice interview. Listen to the interview together and give your child compliments as well as some suggestions for improvement. Then go with him to the real interview.

Variations: Your child could also videotape the interview.

✋ This activity will be fine as written for kinesthetic learners, as they will be able to move around while doing the whole activity.

👁 It would be good for visual learners to videotape the interview to watch later.

👂 This activity will be fine for auditory learners as most of the activity is done orally. Recording the interview also allows your child to go back and listen to the answers again.

Mastery occurs when: your child understands the job responsibilities of the person he interviewed.

You might want to help your child a little more if: he doesn't understand the job responsibilities of the person interviewed. Try listening to the interview again. See if there is a video available that would help him see the job description in action.

2 | Government Bingo

TIME: 30 minutes

MATERIALS
▪ objects to use as markers, such as pennies
▪ list of government terms
▪ dictionary
▪ index cards

Create a bingo card with government terms listed on it, like the one on page 183.

Learning happens when: your child writes the definition on individual index cards for each term on the bingo card. Have your child put one of the markers in the box marked "FREE SPACE." Shuffle the index cards. Draw a card and read the definition aloud. Your child should find the term that goes with the definition on her bingo card and put a marker on that space. Continue with this procedure until your child has covered five spaces in a row. The row can be covered vertically, horizontally, or diagonally.

city manager	ballot	senate	district	state legislature
budget	economy	house of representatives	county	government
election	mayor	FREE SPACE	governor	vote
county seat	state treasurer	city council	candidate	citizen
municipal court	tax	laws	campaign	democrat

Variations: You could put the definitions on the card instead of the vocabulary words.

✍ This activity is good for kinesthetic learners because they are moving and manipulating objects as they play the game.

👁 It might be helpful to let visual learners see the index cards and read them by themselves.

👂 Auditory learners should repeat the definition after you say it and then say the vocabulary word aloud as they cover up the space.

Mastery occurs when: your child can match all of the government vocabulary words with the correct definitions.

You might want to help your child a little more if: she can't find the correct vocabulary word for each definition. Try making a smaller bingo card with fewer vocabulary words. When your child can identify those terms, add more to the card and continue until she can identify all of the words.

3 Mayor for a Day

TIME: 1–2 hours

MATERIALS
- notebook
- pencils

Learning happens when: you arrange for you and your child to spend twenty minutes with your local mayor. (If the mayor or another city official is not available, pretend that you or another family member is the mayor so that your child can learn about the city while gaining some experience interviewing an adult.) Spend time with your child before the interview listing some questions that your child should ask the mayor. Talk about the manners your child should use when interviewing the mayor and how to take notes. When you go with your child to see the mayor, bring along the notebook and list of questions. At the end of the day, have your child write down his thoughts about what he learned.

Variations: Your child could arrange to have you or someone else videotape the interview. He could then show it to his classmates.

✋ Kinesthetic learners can take the interview information and act out what they think the mayor does when running the city.

👁 Visual learners can take the interview information and draw pictures that show what they think the mayor does when running the city.

👂 Auditory learners could tape record the events of the day, listen to the notes, and then tell you or another family member what the mayor does.

Mastery occurs when: your child understands some of the responsibilities of your local mayor.

You might want to help your child a little more if: he does not understand the mayor's job. Try reviewing the notes he took. Explain in more detail and give examples.

4 Local Officials

Learning happens when: Your child records the names of your local officials on a chart like the one below (you can find this and other helpful charts at www.knowledgeessentials.com). You can find the names of your local officials around election time or in issues of your town or city's newspaper that report on city council meetings. You can also find the names on your city's Web site or in materials that you pick up from your local chamber of commerce. You can sometimes find this information on school district maps that you get from your local school board office.

TIME: 30 minutes

MATERIALS

- pencils
- paper

Name of city and state	
Mayor	
City manager	
City council member	
City council member	
City council member	
City council member	
City council member	
City council member	
City treasurer	

Variations: Your child could find out what areas each city council member represents. This information could be recorded on a map or on a chart that you make.

✋ Kinesthetic learners could make a 3-D map or a physical model of the different areas that each city council member represents.

👁 Visual learners might make a map to show each area the city council members represent.

👂 Auditory learners could write a radio announcement about the local government officials.

Mastery occurs when: your child can tell you who the local government officials are for your city.

You might want to help your child a little more if: she can't tell you the names of the local government officials. Try making flashcards to help her remember.

5 | What Needs Doing?

TIME: 20–30 minutes

MATERIALS
▪ notebook
▪ pencils

Learning happens when: you drive or walk with your child around your city looking for things that need to be fixed or things that would make the city better. Have your child write them in a notebook along with an explanation of why the city needs these things to be done (for example, pot holes, traffic signs, park maintenance). Have your child write a letter to the city council members about addressing these needs.

Variations: Your child could also take pictures of the problem areas and send them along with the letter to the city council members.

✋ Kinesthetic learners will do fine with the activity as written because there's plenty of moving around.

👁 It would be good for visual learners to take pictures of the problem areas to send to the city council members.

🦻 Auditory learners could tape record their observations of problem areas.

Mastery occurs when: your child sees how changes are made in the community.

You might want to help your child a little more if: he can't understand the process of improving the community. Try taking him to a city council meeting and explaining what's going on.

6 | Government Hunt

Learning happens when: your child reads the newspaper and cuts out articles that are about the government. After a week or so, help your child take the articles and divide them into three categories: local, state, and national. Take one piece of construction paper or poster board for each category and arrange the articles on them. When your child has arranged the articles in the way she wants, she can glue the articles onto the paper or poster board. Ask your child questions about each set of articles. Make a chart to compare the different categories of government.

Time: 10–20 minutes each day for a week

Materials
▪ newspaper
▪ large sheet of construction paper or poster board
▪ rounded-edge scissors
▪ nontoxic glue

Variations: Your child could also use the Internet to search for information and news articles about government.

✋ Kinesthetic learners will like the activity the way it is because they are manipulating a lot of materials.

👁 Visual learners also will like the activity the way it is because they are making a visual to present the information.

🦻 Auditory learners could tape record their findings.

Mastery occurs when: your child understands some of the responsibilities of each category of government.

You might want to help your child a little more if: she can't tell you some of the responsibilities of each category of government. Try making flash cards with some of the different responsibilities written on them. Use them when you have some free time.

7 Advertisement

Learning happens when: your child pretends to be a candidate for a political office. He must first decide what office he is running for. Read the newspaper to get some ideas about current issues. Then your child should determine what issues he will be for or against. Next, your child needs to plan a short video advertisement using these issues to tell the voters what he stands for. Practice and then have someone videotape the advertisement.

Variations: Your child could also do a radio advertisement or a campaign brochure.

✍ Kinesthetic learners would do fine with any of the variations for the advertisement. All of them allow for some movement.

👁 Visual learners should choose between the video advertisement and the brochure.

👂 Auditory learners would learn best by doing the radio advertisement.

Mastery occurs when: your child understands some of the issues in our world today and takes a stand either for or against them.

You might want to help your child a little more if: he is not able to understand the issues. Try picking a couple of the issues for him and ask him questions to help organize his thoughts and beliefs.

8 | State Government Cluster

TIME: 30 minutes

MATERIALS
- paper
- pencils
- information about your state government (you can find a link to your state's Internet Web site at www .knowledgeessentials.com)

Learning happens when: you and your child read the information about your state government and then organize it into a cluster map. Label the center oval "state government," then draw three ovals around the center oval and connect them to it with a line. In each oval write one of three branches of government: legislative, executive, and judicial. Have your child write information about each branch of government on the lines coming off each oval. Be sure your child has written down who is in charge of each branch and the main responsibilities of each branch. Then your child can use the cluster map to give an oral report about the state government.

Environmental Learning

Your child can learn a lot about his or her community, region, and local government by reading newspapers and watching the news on television. See if you can find your child a pen pal from a different region of the United States. If possible, take a vacation to a different region so your child can personally experience it. Have your child write a letter to the governor or some other official in your community. Model being a good citizen for your child. Be involved at school and in the community. Take part in local elections by discussing the issues at home and then voting.

End of Fourth Grade Social Studies Checklist

Students who are working at the standard level at the end of fourth grade:

____ Can identify the five regions of the United States

____ Know basic information about the climate, landforms, natural resources, industries, and major cities in each of the five regions

____ Can name the states and their capitals

____ Know how to use different types of maps to learn about the United States

____ Know the political leaders of the city in which they live

____ Know the political leaders of the state in which they live

Teaching Your Fourth Grader Thinking Skills

10

> **Beginning of Fourth Grade Thinking Skills Checklist**
>
> Students who are working at the standard level at the beginning of fourth grade:
>
> _____ Think chronologically
>
> _____ Begin to use thinking processes (writing process)
>
> _____ Consider and choose problem-solving strategies
>
> _____ Begin to think in abstract terms
>
> _____ Can relate previous knowledge to new knowledge

Teaching your fourth grader to think sounds like a lofty goal, doesn't it? You can help foster a thinking mind in your child by treating him or her as an active participant in a home where you explore "why" and "how" questions. The more opportunities your child has to explore ideas and be heard at home, the more likely he or she is to be an active thinker both in and out of school.

Teaching children to think reasonably and logically improves children's impulsive behavior and social adjustment. Children taught this way are less likely to develop behavioral difficulties than are well-adjusted children who do not learn these skills. Of course, the way you respond to your child and act in front of him or her makes the largest impact on how your child learns to think and communicate.

In a study of children from kindergarten through fourth grade (Shure, 1993) that was the culmination of twenty years of research to test ideas about thinking skills, parent modeling, and behavior, M. B. Shure delineated four levels of communication that we use all the time:

LEVEL 1: POWER ASSERTION (DEMANDS, BELITTLES, PUNISHES)

- Do it because I say so!
- Do you want a time out?
- How many times have I told you . . . !
- If you can't share the truck, I'll take it away so that neither of you will have it.

LEVEL 2: POSITIVE ALTERNATIVE (NO EXPLANATION)

- I'm on the phone now. Go watch TV.
- Ask him for the truck.
- You should share your toys.

LEVEL 3: INDUCTION (EXPLANATIONS AND REASONS)

- I feel angry when you interrupt me.
- If you hit, you'll lose a friend (hurt him).
- You'll make him angry if you hit him (grab toys).
- You shouldn't hit (grab). It's not nice.

LEVEL 4: PROBLEM-SOLVING PROCESS (TEACHING THINKING)

- What's the problem? What's the matter?
- How do you think I (she/he) feel(s) when you hit (grab)?
- What happened (might happen) when you did (do) that?
- Can you think of a different way to solve this problem (tell him/her/me how you feel)?
- Do you think that is or is not a good idea? Why (why not)?

The parents who communicated as often as possible on level 4 in Shure's study had children who were the least impulsive, the least withdrawn, and showed the fewest behavior problems as observed by independent raters.

We all know that there are times when communicating on level 1 is the only way to go, so don't beat yourself up. You can't reason a child out of the street when a car is coming. Awareness of the communication levels enables you to implement the highest level as much of the time as possible, which in turn fosters a thinking child.

Teaching and modeling thinking encourages children to ask questions about information and ideas. It helps your child learn how to identify unstated assumptions, form and defend opinions, and see relationships between events and ideas. A thinking person raises a thinking child. That you are even reading this book assures you are a thinking person, so you are on the right track.

Don't expect your child's fourth grade teacher to stand up in front of the class and say "Okay, it's time to learn to think." Instead, your child's teacher will incorporate activities and language that foster the development and refinement of thinking skills, such as problem solving, concentration, and reasoning, throughout your child's daily activities. In the same way, you will foster thinking skills if you do many of the activities in this book with your child.

There are many approaches to teaching thinking. You can teach your child to use a set of identifiable skills, such as deciding between relevant and irrelevant information and generating questions from written material. This is particularly useful for auditory and visual learners. Your kinesthetic child learns to think more actively by participating in sports, hands-on projects, and similar activities.

Problem Solving

Problem solving is a hallmark of mathematical activity and a major means of developing mathematical knowledge. It is finding a way to reach a goal that is not immediately attainable. Problem solving is natural to young children because the world is new to them, and they exhibit curiosity, intelligence, and flexibility as they face new situations.

The challenge at this level is to build on children's innate problem-solving inclinations and to preserve and encourage a disposition that values problem solving. Try the problem-solving math section in chapter 7 and the science activities about systems in chapter 8 as challenging opportunities for your child.

Concentration

Thinking skills begin with the ability to maintain a focus on one thing long enough to think it through. Thinking something through means understanding the information (in whatever form—for example, visual, print, or oral), questioning the information, and thinking about the alternatives before making a decision.

Concentration skills are a big part of learning to read. Your child's teacher will be working hard with him or her on concentration skills, and you can help reinforce these skills by trying the activities in the reading comprehension section of chapter 5.

Comprehension

This is a hard one. To think about something in a reasonable, logical manner, you need to understand it, but creative thinking is born from instances where you don't understand something. The trick is probably in the mix. Let your child explore new information and form creative thoughts about it, then talk to him or her logically about it. Giving your child time to think freely about new information allows him or her to think about it in many contexts and many forms before being told which concept or form is proper.

In order to better develop your child's understanding of different concepts, his or her perception should be shaped by touching, hearing, and seeing something simultaneously, to experience the concept as best as he or she can. Take time to let your child talk about what he or she is seeing, touching, and hearing. By experiencing new concepts in different contexts, your child can become aware of different aspects of an idea and develop his or her understanding of its meaning.

Reasoning

There is more than one type of reasoning. Formal reasoning skills, such as deductive and inductive reasoning, are developed at a later age. The reasoning skill that is focused on in fourth grade is spatial-temporal reasoning, or the ability to visualize and transform objects in space.

Spatial-temporal operations are responsible for combining separate elements of an object into a single whole, or for arranging objects in a specific spatial order. Spatial-temporal operations require successive steps; each step is dependent on previous ones.

Spatial-temporal skills are the most frequently tested reasoning/thinking skills on IQ and other standardized tests. You can work on these skills with your child through the math and science activities in this book.

Logic

Children learn about and understand logical concepts in different ways. In math, for example, some kids think about numbers in terms of where they are on a number line, while other kids think about how many objects make up each number. These children reach an understanding of numbers, their meaning, and how to use them, but they reach it in different ways. Taking this example further, these children comprehend the information and understand what numbers represent. But if one group is then asked to handle the numbers in different contexts, the group will need to be aware of different aspects of numbers in order to develop a fuller understanding of their meaning. The group can then think about numbers in different ways and apply them to different situations in a logical way rather than simply recall what they mean.

A large part of logical thinking stems from the ability to see objects and apply concepts in many contexts (spatial-temporal reasoning applies here). Teaching children to question information teaches them to think about the information in more than one context before making a logical conclusion about it. Logical thinking can be reinforced during the discipline process by applying logical consequences to a behavior rather than using an arbitrary punishment.

Thinking Skills Activities

To help your child develop thinking skills, you can:

- Encourage her to ask questions about the world around her.
- Ask him to imagine what will happen next in the story when you are reading together.
- Actively listen to your child's conversation, responding seriously and nonjudgmentally to her questions.
- Ask what he is feeling and why when he expresses feelings.
- Suggest that she find facts to support her opinions, and encourage her to locate information relevant to her opinions.
- Use entertainment—a book, a TV program, or a movie—as the basis of family discussions.
- Use daily activities as occasions for learning (environmental learning).
- Reward him for inquisitive and/or creative activity that is productive.
- Ask her what she learned at school.

Environmental Learning

There are thousands of ways that you can use your child's everyday environment to encourage thinking skills. Remember, if your child is an active participant in a home where there are "why" and "how" discussions, he or she is more likely to be an active thinker both in and out of school.

End of Fourth Grade Thinking Skills Checklist

Students who are working at the standard level at the end of fourth grade:

_____ Feel comfortable using symbolic reasoning

_____ Use thinking processes in multiple subject areas (the writing process, the scientific process, math properties)

_____ Think independently

_____ Can transfer thinking from one situation to another

Assessment

11

A key component to learning is evaluating what has been learned. Assessment serves several different purposes:

1. Assessing individual student abilities and knowledge and adapting instructions accordingly

2. Evaluating and improving the instructional program in general

3. Determining individual student eligibility for promotion or graduation, college admission, or special honors

4. Measuring and comparing school, school district, statewide, and national performance for broad public accountability

There is more than one kind of assessment and more than one context in which this term is frequently used. There are multiple ways that you and your child's teacher assess your child. There is broad assessment of your child's knowledge of certain things and his performance as compared to other children of the same age and grade. Standardized assessment is usually done at the end of the year and comprises many sessions of test taking in a short time period. There are uses for all types of assessment.

Assessing Individual Student Abilities and Knowledge

Students learn in different ways, so teachers assess their daily learning in different ways. The most common way to assess daily learning is by observing how your child responds to and implements things that he or she learns in the classroom. As teachers observe and consider the variety of daily assignments of students, they begin to help their students demonstrate this learning on tests.

Observation and Portfolio Assessment

Your child's overall progress is assessed by considering her developmental stage and cognitive learning abilities with key concepts and key skills within the framework of her learning styles. Teachers (and by now, you) do this by observing your child on a daily basis, giving basic skills tests, gauging reaction and comprehension time when given new information, and asking frequent, informal questions. All of the activities in this book include explanations for how to assess your child's performance, and the checklists at the beginning and end of the chapters can help you assess your child's progress in each skill.

Teachers have begun to implement portfolio assessment more frequently. Teachers are giving your child the opportunity to demonstrate learning through a variety of activities, such as art projects, writing activities, oral presentations, and daily participation with unit tests, to determine the true levels of comprehension and skill development with the variety of materials and skills in each learning unit. Many people think portfolio assessment is one of the most accurate methods of determining learning, but it can be subjective, so it has been criticized. Teachers try really hard not to be subjective; contrary to what some people think, they aren't likely to retaliate for a mishap with a parent by lowering the child's grades. When a child succeeds, the teacher has also succeeded. Discounting the child's success because of personal feelings destroys the teacher's professional success.

Always remember (even if your child does really well) that achievement tests are just one measure of your child's learning. You know this is true because you have been using rough measures in the activities you do with your child. Observation is a primary assessment tool.

Standardized Testing

Testing is a hot topic, and rightly so. We all remember the standardized tests—spending days filling in little circles with a number 2 pencil.

The majority of teachers dislike standardized testing for a number of reasons. Sure, there is the issue of accountability. But the heart of the issue is not that teachers are afraid of being held to a standard to keep their job—it is that they disagree with being held to what many of them believe is a false standard. Think about how an auditory or physical learner will do on a test designed for visual learners. The tests aren't an accurate picture of what all learners can do.

In defense of test makers, they are doing their best to adjust their approaches within the limitations of state requirements, logistical requirements, and traditional business practices. But the system within which teachers, parents, students, and test makers are trying to operate is definitely imperfect.

Others' issues are centered around "teaching the test." Teachers are afraid the curriculum they are told to teach will be so narrowly geared toward the test that it will limit their ability to teach the things that support the tested items. They are concerned they will only be able to teach to the cognitive learning level when they know the student should also be able to apply the knowledge, synthesize it, and evaluate it. We have discussed how individual scores can be invalid, but so can group scores. Test results may be invalidated by teaching so narrowly to the objectives of a particular test that scores are raised without actually improving the broader, often more important, set of academic skills that the test should be measuring.

At the end of the day, assessment is a very strong tool. It encourages, discourages, and measures learning. Assessment should be a means of fostering growth toward high expectations and should support student learning. When assessments are used in thoughtful and meaningful ways and combined with information from other sources, students' scores provide important information that can lead to decisions that promote student learning and equality of opportunity. The misuse of tests for high-stakes purposes (tests that are used to make significant educational decisions about children, teachers, schools, or school districts) has undermined the benefits these tests can foster.

The standardized tests that cause so much controversy are norm-referenced tests, meaning the test questions are selected so that a national sample of students' test scores will result in a normal distribution: there will always be a group of students at the bottom, a majority in the middle, and a group at the top. It is unrealistic to expect whole groups of students to be in the top percentiles (or groups) on these tests. Most students are expected to perform near the fiftieth percentile.

Helping Your Child Test Well

You play a vital role in helping your child succeed on standardized tests. Here are just a few things you can do:

- Put your child at ease by discussing your own experiences with taking tests. If you were nervous or anxious, talk about it. Let him know those feelings are normal.

- Be aware of the specific days tests will be given. Ask your child how the testing sessions are going. Offer encouragement.

- Stress the importance of listening to test directions and following them carefully. Provide practice activities at home, such as following a recipe or reading and answering questions about a story.

- Make sure your child goes to bed early every night and at the same time every night, especially on the night before testing.

- Encourage healthy eating, rest, and exercise.

- Most standardized testing is given over a three- or four-day period. Ask your child's teacher for a schedule, and make sure your child attends school on those days.

- Meet with your child's teachers to discuss the results. If your child had difficulty in specific areas, ask teachers for suggestions in the form of homework assignments, techniques, and specific material.

What the Scores Really Mean

High-stakes tests are used to make significant educational decisions about children, teachers, schools, or school districts. To use a single objective test in the determination of such things as graduation, course credit, grade placement, promotion to the next grade, or placement in special groups is a serious misuse of tests. Remember, your child's score on a standardized test is only one measure of what he knows. Most schools use multiple measures, including student projects, homework, portfolios, chapter tests, and oral reports.

Measuring and Comparing School, School District, Statewide, and National Performance for Broad Public Accountability

Increasingly, policy makers at the federal, state, and local levels want to identify ways to measure student performance in order to see how well the public education system is doing its job. The goals of this accountability approach include providing information about the status of the educational system, motivating desired change, measuring program effectiveness, and creating systems for rewarding and sanctioning educators based on the performance of their students.

The use of testing to change classroom instruction is central to the theory of standards-based reform. It assumes that educators and the public can agree on what should be taught; that a set of clear standards can be developed, which in turn drive curriculum and instruction; and that tests can measure how well students perform based on those standards.

Fourth Grade Society   12

Fourth grade is the beginning of the end of childhood. Your child will hit a double digit age, and the next six years—the critical ones between wanting independence and achieving it—can be frustratingly great. Your child is developing into a teenager and facets of that personality are popping up at odd times. Go with it—but only after preparing for it. This chapter should help make the road a little smoother.

Ten Going on Thirty

Fourth graders are a unique mixture of childlike innocence and blossoming maturity. Your child is officially in the "tween" years—teetering between childhood and early adolescence—and it confuses everyone. One minute you are buying Barbie dolls for your daughter, the next minute you are trying to stop her from wearing colored lip gloss. Your child's most common response to anything you ever suggest is, "I'm too old for that!" Tweens today may play like children at home but can instantly transform themselves into sophisticated adults for a trip to the mall. They have outgrown the bright primary colors and the cartoon motifs with which you so lovingly decorated their rooms, and only play with dolls or race cars behind closed doors. These young people have their own ideas and desires. "Tweens" still need special interactions with their parents, sometimes more than they are willing to admit.

Finding the right kind of interaction can be difficult. Kids this age are eager for new adventures and to make their own decisions. Parents of tweens need to strengthen the bonds with their children and let them know that they are available to them. It is important to find activities for you and your child that will stimulate positive relationships and healthy growth. It is equally important that the positive relationship between you and your child foster healthy expression of the independent thoughts your child is having. Your children don't have to be just like you for you to enjoy them, so welcome their unique expression of your similarities.

When your child is ready for a little more independence get into a routine of hanging out together, then separating for a defined period of time that your child can get used to being with his or her friends before meeting you at a designated spot. You can apply this method to many activities that your child would like to begin doing alone, but that you feel that he or she is just a little too young for. Movies are a great example. Get tickets for yourself to a movie you want to see at a multiplex so that your child can go with his or her friends to see a different movie at the same theater. You can control certain aspects of the event while giving your child the freedom to be with his or her friends.

As children seesaw back and forth between childhood and adolescence, you need to be flexible enough to recognize what your child is feeling and respond accordingly. Ask yourself, "Is he ready for this? Am I ready for this?" Each time you loosen the reins and let your child take a new step, it is natural to experience your own doubts and ambivalence until the new situation is mastered and/or the new rules are established. Your job as a parent requires you to maintain both a healthy apprehension for your child's safety and well-being, while encouraging him or her to develop new skills and autonomy. It's a tough balance, but I am certain you are up to it.

The Green-Eyed Monster

Late elementary school can bring forth your child's first real encounter with jealousy in the outside world, which is different from being jealous of a brother or sister. With a brother or sister, there is a permanence to the relationship that is a boundary to how far out of hand the jealousy gets. At the end of the day brothers and sisters are brothers and sisters and that alone can be a stop-gap between minor and out-of-hand jealousy.

Situations where your child may feel jealous or may experience another's jealousy include:

- Academic or physical performance. Sometimes friends can be a little competitive with each other, whether it is in the classroom or on the playground. Sometimes friends can feel a little jealous if one outperforms the other. If your child is feeling jealous toward a friend, it may help to reassure your child that friends balance each other. Each person has strengths and weaknesses; your child can do things the other cannot, and vice versa. On the other hand, if your child's friend is acting in a jealous way toward your child, you can help your child deal with it by reassuring the friend and pointing out his strengths.

- The third wheel. Sometimes jealousy can result from a third person. Because of the growing importance of friendship, some fourth graders will feel threatened by a friend's other friendships. If your child is feeling jealous about a friend's other friendships, empathize, but help your child put it in perspective: another friendship does not diminish the importance of your child's friendship, and making a friend choose is not fair. Your child cares about many people. Ask your child to imagine one of those people demanding that your child stop caring about all the other people and only care about her. It would not be fair, because all those people are important to your child. The same can be said for her friend. If your child's friend is acting with jealousy concerning your child's other friendships, help your child to handle that. Remind your child that a jealous friend wants to know she is important. See if the jealous friend will agree that everyone can be friends. Generally, a fourth grader would be happy with that. Occasionally, a jealous friend may make an ultimatum. It can be agonizing to a fourth grader to feel that she must make a choice between friends. Help your child understand that the jealous friend is being unfair, and to resist breaking a friendship to appease that person.

Homework!

Are you flabbergasted about the amount of homework your child is getting at such an early age? Don't be. There are several reasons why your child should have homework:

- To review information learned that day
- To practice old skills
- To practice new skills
- To complete unfinished class work
- To study for tests
- To complete long-term projects, such as reports

Homework promotes good study habits and organizational skills. You child should gradually become accustomed to planning and scheduling his or her time so that all needs, wants, and obligations are satisfied. Homework also gives you an opportunity to participate in your child's learning.

Most school nights, fourth grade students should be able to finish their homework in thirty minutes to an hour. If your child is spending more than an hour each evening on homework, you should contact his or her homeroom teacher to talk about why it may be taking so long.

Homework is expected to be done when it is assigned, but don't let your child get too stressed out about deadlines. Most assignments are to be completed in one evening and turned in the next day. Some homework projects, such as reports, will take several days to complete. For long-term assignments, due dates will always be provided by the teacher so children will know exactly when the assignment is due and how long they have to complete the work.

To help your child avoid homework-related stress, you can effectively manage his or her time. Talk to your child about how long it usually takes him or her to complete homework assignments and how he or she can find the time to do a long-term project by using that time spread across several nights. The following are some helpful suggestions for getting homework done:

- Use car time to quiz your child on homework.

- Create a comfortable environment where your child can do his or her homework.

- Have a set daily routine for homework.

- Make sure the TV set is turned off while your child is doing his or her homework.

By the second month of school you should see a homework pattern emerge: a little math every night, spelling lists every Monday, and so forth. Look for the pattern and keep track of it. The following are four strategies to keeping calm and staying organized during the school year:

1. Check your child's backpack each evening for school notices and notes from the teacher.

2. Have your child pack his backpack before going to bed each evening.

3. Your child's teacher may have given your child a homework planner. Make sure to check it to be sure your child is keeping it up-to-date. If your child doesn't have a planner already, get her one

and work with your child until she uses it effectively. Go over the things your child wrote in the planner every day.

4. Keep a separate calendar for school events, homework deadlines, and other important dates.

When your child wants help with homework, there are things you can do that don't mean doing the work yourself:

- Ask your child if he understands the homework. If he does not, work on a few examples together, then let him do the rest alone.

- Ask to see your child's homework after the teacher returns it, to learn where she is having trouble and where she is doing well.

- Don't be afraid to get in touch with the teacher if you and your child don't understand an assignment or if your child is having a great deal of trouble.

Homework doesn't have to be the worst thing in the world. Remember to praise your child for doing well and keep a portfolio of "best pieces." Your visions of a nightly battle will fade if you set a routine, check the backpack, and work on time management, and homework will be a breeze.

Moving On to Fifth Grade

You made it! Your fourth grader is now going to be a fifth grader, and you are going to be the parent of a fifth grader!

You can monitor your child's readiness for fifth grade and determine areas that you can help your child reinforce with the following subject area and developmental checklists.

Ready to Go

Students who are ready to go on to fifth grade:

Reading

_____ Read with understanding and fluency

_____ Use graphic organizers to aid comprehension

_____ Visualize descriptions and details

_____ Can follow and give sequential directions

_____ Can summarize a story

_____ Can use past experiences to identify with a character

_____ Compare and contrast various things

_____ Understand cause and effect relationships

_____ Can use basic rules with quotation marks in dialogue

Writing

_____ Use the writing process to compose

_____ Use various sentence types appropriately

_____ Use both simple and compound sentence structures

_____ Understand the parts of a sentence

_____ Use a broader vocabulary to express themselves

_____ Write in cursive neatly and consistently

_____ Recognize and use proper punctuation

Math

_____ Discover, describe, and extend geometric and number patterns

_____ Solve simple math sentences that contain a variable

_____ Read, write, and rename whole numbers through millions

_____ Read, write, and rename decimals to the hundreds

_____ Compare and order whole numbers and decimals

_____ Explore equivalent and nonequivalent fractions and begin to compare, add, and subtract them

_____ Multiply larger numbers

_____ Learn long division

_____ Begin developing mental math ability and estimation skills

_____ Know the basic characteristics of lines and angles

_____ Can establish measurement benchmarks

_____ Collect, record, and analyze data to investigate probability

Science

____ Begin to use scientific methods

____ Can identify pushing and pulling as a means to change the position of an object

____ Understand closed and open electric circuits

____ Understand how matter is changed by adding or reducing heat

____ Can identify adaptive characteristics in organisms

____ Know the needs of organisms that must be met in their environment

____ Can classify organisms and understand the roles of organisms in living systems

____ Can distinguish between inherited and learned traits

____ Can identify the effects of weathering, erosion, and sedimentation

Social Studies

____ Can identify the five regions of the United States

____ Know basic information about the climate, landforms, natural resources, industries, and major cities in each of the five regions

____ Can name the states and their capitals

____ Know how to use different types of maps to learn about the United States

____ Know the political leaders of the city in which they live

____ Know the political leaders of the state in which they live

Thinking Skills

____ Feel comfortable using symbolic reasoning

____ Use thinking processes in multiple subject areas (the writing process, the scientific process, math properties)

____ Think independently

____ Can transfer thinking from one situation to another

LITERATURE FOR FOURTH GRADERS

This section contains a list of books that your child may find interesting, and learning activities along with the reading selections. You can find more recommended literature for your fourth grader at www .knowledgeessentials.com.

Fly Away Home

Author: Eve Bunting
Publisher: Clarion Books

This picture book is about a boy and his dad who live in an airport. The boy is telling their story about being homeless. They are trying to make the best of the situation and are always looking for a way out. It also describes the things they do so as not to be noticed.

Special Considerations: Because this is a sensitive subject, it would be best to read this book with your child.

Learning: How can we help people who are homeless? What types of services are available to them in our community?

Activity: Let your child participate in donating food or clothing to an agency. Maybe he could serve meals at one of the local shelters.

Follow Up: Have your child research how many homeless people there are in your community. Do the same thing for your state as well as the United States. Graph the results.

Dear Mr. Henshaw
Author: Beverly Cleary
Publisher: William Morrow

A boy writes letters to his favorite author about the problems in his life. Most of these problems are a result of his parents' divorce. Mr. Henshaw's response ends up helping the boy.

Special Considerations: This book addresses a sensitive subject for young children. Many children have either gone through a divorce or know someone who has. Your child should be able to read this on her own, but you might want to discuss it with her afterward.

Learning: This is a good book for learning letter-writing skills. It's also good for discussing the feelings children have when they go through a divorce and how it affects them.

Activity: Have your child write a letter to her favorite author.

Follow Up: Ask your child to make a list of the things she would like to know about her favorite author, then research the author to find the answers to the questions.

Pinballs
Author: Betsy Byars
Publisher: HarperCollins

Three foster children come to live with the Mason family. They are there because of physical abuse and abandonment. The story mainly deals with the problems foster children have in learning to trust others.

Special Considerations: Your child should be able to read this book on his own. However, there are some references to entertainers from the past about whom he might need your help. Foster care can also be a sensitive subject for young children.

Learning: Children can learn how to compromise with others. What is the foster care system? Who can be a foster parent?

Activity: The children in this story compare themselves to a pinball game. Have your child compare his life to a different game. Discuss how some part of his life is a part of the game.

Follow Up: Have your child use a Venn diagram to compare his own life to the life of a foster child.

Sign of the Beaver

Author: Elizabeth George Speare
Publisher: Houghton Mifflin

The story is set in eighteenth-century Maine. A young boy is left alone in his family's cabin as his father goes back to Massachusetts to get the rest of the family. The boy has an incident with bees, ends up getting stung many times, and is helped by a Native American boy. He makes friends with the boy and the boy's grandfather.

Special Considerations: Your child should be able to read this on her own. You might have to help her with some of the vocabulary words, especially the ones from the Indian language.

Learning: List what family life was like in this time period. How did they get their basic needs? Locate on a map the states in which the story takes place.

Activity: Have your child make a chart that compares and contrasts the settlers' way of life and the Native Americans' way of life.

Follow Up: The boy uses the alphabet to help teach the Native American boy to read. Have your child create an ABC book that relates to things from *Sign of the Beaver*.

On My Honor

Author: Marion Dane Bauer
Publisher: Yearling

Joel and his best friend Tony spend all of their time together. They get permission to ride their bikes to Starved Rock, but they get sidetracked and end up going by a dangerous river. Tony ends up drowning, and the rest of the story deals with Joel's feelings of guilt and sadness as he tries to deal with the death of his best friend.

Special Considerations: Your child should be able to read this book on his own. If he has recently lost a friend or a loved one, however, you might want to read it with him.

Learning: Learn about swimming safety in both pools and rivers. You can also use this book to discuss peer pressure.

Activity: Have your child make a poster that shows what safety procedures should be followed when swimming in a pool or a river.

Follow Up: Take a class on CPR with your child.

How to Eat Fried Worms

Author: Thomas Rockwell
Publisher: Yearling

If Billy eats fifteen worms in fifteen days he will win fifty dollars. Billy can cook the worms or even put things on them. This funny story describes the ways Billy prepares the worms and the things his friend does to try to keep him from winning the bet.

Special Considerations: Your child should be able to read this book on her own.

Learning: What is proper nutrition? Could a worm provide any of those nutrients? Is it wise to take a bet?

Activity: Have your child find a recipe in a recipe book. Discuss the measurement units that are used.

Follow Up: Help your child plan a balanced meal.

Wait Till Helen Comes
Author: Mary Downing Hahn
Publisher: Clarion Books

This is a ghost story about a family that moves into a church that has been converted into a home. Molly and Michael do not get along with their new stepsister, Heather. Heather becomes friends with a ghost and tells her stepbrother and stepsister about it, but they don't believe her. When Heather's life is put in danger because of the ghost, Molly and Michael must put aside their feelings to save her.

Special Considerations: Your child should be able to read this book on his own, but it is a ghost story, so if your child gets scared easily you may want to monitor him while he is reading this book.

Learning: Since the story is about blended families, this would be a good time to discuss the feelings that come up when two families join into one. What causes these feelings? What could the families do to help make the blending of the families easier?

Activity: Have your child go through the story and list the words that help to make the story scary. Also have him write the part of speech for each word as it is used in the sentence.

Follow Up: Using some of the scary words from the activity, have your child write his own ghost story.

Ramona the Pest

Author: Beverly Cleary
Publisher: William Morrow

Ramona is a five-year-old entering kindergarten. She is curious and always needs to know what will happen next. She usually loves her teachers and school. Then something happens that almost makes Ramona a kindergarten dropout. The story tells about the day-to-day life of a kindergartner in a hilarious way.

Special Considerations: Your child should be able to read this book without any help.

Learning: What is it like to start school for the first time? What kinds of things did we learn in kindergarten? How is fourth grade similar to and different from kindergarten?

Activity: Have your child write a short essay on the similarities and differences between kindergarten and fourth grade.

Follow Up: Help your child baby-sit a child of kindergarten age. Plan some appropriate activities to do with him or her.

The Castle in the Attic

Author: Elizabeth Winthrop
Publisher: Holiday House

William's nanny, Mrs. Phillips, is moving back to England. As a going-away gift she gives William a miniature castle and a knight. The Silver Knight comes to life and wants William to help regain control of his kingdom. In the meantime, with the help of a magic medal, William shrinks Mrs. Phillips and puts her in the castle. William himself is shrunk and enters the kingdom to help the Silver Knight get his kingdom back.

Special Considerations: Your child should be able to read this book on her own, although there are a lot of vocabulary words dealing with the castle about which she might need your help.

Learning: What is a fantasy book? What is chivalry?

Activity: List the things in this book that make it a fantasy. Go to the library and check out another fantasy book to read.

Follow Up: Have your child write her own fantasy story and share it with someone else. Visit a museum to see a knight's armor.

Stuart Little

Author: E. B. White

Publisher: HarperTrophy

Stuart Little is a mouse who is born to a human family, the Littles. As Stuart learns to fit into his human family he has many adventures, such as becoming friends with the family cat, Snowbell, which is not an easy task. Stuart has many small jobs that only a small mouse can do (retrieving a ring from a drain, fixing a piano key).

He makes friends with a beautiful bird named Margalo. When Margalo goes missing he vows to find his best friend. This is the first time Stuart has ever been away from home. He has many adventures as he tries to find Margalo. These adventures help him to grow and mature. Stuart doesn't find Margalo, but he knows someday he will see his friend again.

Learning: What did we learn about being a good friend? How can we be helpful to our friends? Who can help us if we lose a pet?

Special Considerations: Your child should be able to read this book on his own although there will be words that he will need help with.

Activity: Have your child make a map of your community that includes your home, your school, any parks, and any buildings that have community helpers who can help you if he loses his pet. These might include the animal shelter or the police station.

Have your child make a flyer you could hang up around your community or an ad that you can put in the community paper to let people know that he has lost his pet. Be sure to have him include a description of the pet, the pet's name, and where you can be reached if someone finds your pet.

Follow up: Find the local animal shelter and take a tour. Have your child help a friend find a lost pet.

SOFTWARE FOR FOURTH GRADERS

Are you eager to use your computer as a learning tool? I bet you told yourself that educational software is the real reason you needed to get the upgraded media package. Here is the chance to redeem yourself. This appendix provides a list of software titles that are appropriate and interesting for fourth grade learners. Since your child may be more adept at the technical portion of the activity, it is not listed. If all else fails, refer to the software's user guide. You can find more recommended computer resources for your fourth grader at www.knowledgeessentials.com.

Kidspiration 2
Inspiration Software

Kidspiration includes standards-based learning activities and templates to help children from kindergarten through fifth grade develop and improve basic skills as well as higher-level thinking skills. It aids children in creating their own graphic organizers that help them categorize, summarize, and synthesize in all subject areas. The curriculum includes activities in the areas of math, analysis, critical thinking, reading, writing, science, and social studies.

Amazon Trail 3rd Edition

The Learning Company

Amazon Trail helps children build real-life skills in decision making and problem solving as they navigate the Amazon River on a wild rainforest adventure. They will experience the mysteries of the rainforest as they build their understanding of history and science.

Cluefinders 4th Grade Adventures—Deluxe 2-CD Set— Puzzles of the Pyramid

The Learning Company

Children solve a thrilling mystery in ancient Egypt and build essential fourth grade skills. They will journey to exotic Egypt on an archaeological dig with the ClueFinders. The mission: to uncover a sinister plot to unleash a dangerous ancient force upon the world. Activities include building a bridge and interpreting mysterious scrolls.

Galswin 4th Grade Reading

Galswin

An award-winning "Play 'n' Learn" collection. You and your child can build learning activities with the Galswin creation module. There are over fifty hours of activities.

Galswin 4th Grade Math

Galswin

An award-winning "Play 'n' Learn" collection with three adventures, including thousands of math exercises.

JumpStart 4th Grade Deluxe

Knowledge Adventure

A two-CD set that teaches essential fourth grade skills. On disc 1, children can rescue a stolen map, catch a villain, and discover lost treasure. On disc 2, children join the JumpStart team and snowboard, inline skate, mountain bike, and rock climb their way through extreme action.

Cluefinders Math Adventures Ages 9–12

The Learning Company

Children build a bevy of math skills as they trek high in the Himalayas with the ClueFinders, who are on a quest to find missing ancient treasures. From purchasing supplies in the village store to building a yak corral, every activity is a math-learning challenge. With fifteen interactive learning games and exercises at ten different skill levels, the software helps to build more than twenty-five key math skills, including number computation, fractions and decimals, tables and graphs, and early geometry.

Cluefinders Reading Adventures Ages 9–12

The Learning Company

The activities are drills for the following reading skills: comprehension, spelling, vocabulary (including synonyms, antonyms, and homonyms), and grammar (including parts of speech and sentence structure). In addition, general critical thinking skills, such as problem solving, hypothesis testing, analogies, and categories, are strengthened in this adventure. Kids must complete each activity multiple times to earn the clues needed to progress in the program.

Quantum Pad Library: Smart Guide to 4th Grade

Leapfrog

Fun, interactive games teach your fourth grader important school subjects. The essential math, science, social studies, and language-arts skills in this guide are correlated to state and national educational standards. Kids just place the book on the Quantum Pad player, pop in the cartridge, and touch any page with the interactive pen to bring learning to life. This book also works with the LeapPad Learning System and the LeapPad Plus Writing Learning System.

Quantum Pad Library: World Geography

Leapfrog

A simple turn of the page sends your child on learning adventures to every corner of the globe. Fun games teach map-reading skills and fascinating facts about our world. It's like an interactive globe for the Quantum Pad Learning System. Kids just place the book on the Quantum Pad player, pop in the cartridge, and touch any page with the interactive pen to bring learning to life. This book also works with the LeapPad Learning System and the LeapPad Plus Writing Learning System.

FOURTH GRADE TOPICAL CALENDAR

This calendar tells you approximately when the skills covered in this book occur during the school year. There will be variances, of course, but for the most part the skills build on one another, so it is logical that your child will learn things in a certain order.

Reading	Writing	Math	Science	Social Studies
September				
Review parts of a story	Review cursive writing mechanics	Place value	Measurement	landforms
Summarize stories	Review sentence formation and punctuation	Compare and order whole numbers	Read charts, tables, and graphs	
Sequential directions		Patterns		
		Variables		
October				
Graphic organizers	Cursive handwriting	Estimate sums and differences	Classification by two or more properties	Regions of the United States
Sequential directions	Parts of a sentence	Addition and sub-traction review	Serial order	
		Review of basic multiplication facts	Scientific method	

Reading	Writing	Math	Science	Social Studies
November				
Parts of a story: characters Read dialogue Summarize stories	Cursive handwriting Parts of a sentence Punctuate dialogue	Estimate products Multiply larger numbers	Physical science • Position and motion • Electricity, closed circuits, and open circuits	Read a variety of maps Regions of the United States
December				
Relate previous knowledge to character experiences Read dialogue Summarize stories	Cursive handwriting Parts of a sentence Punctuate dialogue	Multiply larger numbers Review of basic division facts	Physical science • Changes in matter by adding and reducing heat	Read a variety of maps Regions of the United States Landforms in different regions
January				
Compare and contrast characters Summarize stories	Cursive handwriting Parts of a sentence Poetry	Long division	Life science • Organisms and their roles in living systems	Purpose of city government
February				
Cause-and-effect relationships Relate previous knowledge to cause-and-effect relationships Summarize stories	Cursive handwriting Parts of a sentence Poetry	Decimals Fractions	Life science • Environments and how they meet the needs of organisms	Structure of city government

Reading	Writing	Math	Science	Social Studies
March				
Parts of a story: visualize setting Summarize stories	Cursive handwriting Parts of a sentence Short reports	Lines and angles Coordinate graphs Measurement benchmarks	Life science • Classify organisms • Inherited traits and learned traits	Benefits of city government Participate in city government
April				
Summarize stories Relate setting to previous knowledge	Cursive handwriting Parts of a sentence	Estimate measurements Use tools to measure Area, perimeter, and volume Time and temperature	Earth science • Weathering, erosion, and sedimentation	City government: political campaigns
May				
Summarize stories	Cursive handwriting Parts of a sentence	Pose and answer questions about tables, charts, and graphs Collect, organize, and record information Investigate probability through dice, coins, and spinners	Earth science • Fossils	City government: political campaigns

GLOSSARY

accountability   Holding students responsible for what they learn and teachers responsible for what they teach.

achievement test   A test designed to efficiently measure the amount of knowledge and/or skill a person has acquired. This helps evaluate student learning in comparison with a standard or norm.

acute angle   An angle that is less than 90°.

adaptive characteristics   Traits about an organism that allow it to easily adapt to a new climate, skill, or situation.

adjective   A word that modifies a noun or describes a quality of a person, place, or thing.

adverb   A word that describes a verb, adjective, or another adverb. It often ends in "ly."

air pressure   The pressure exerted by the atmosphere.

antonym   A word that has an opposite meaning of another word.

area   A measure of a surface with boundaries; for example, a square or a triangle. Area is measured in square units.

assessment   Measuring a student's learning.

associative property of multiplication   A regrouping of three or more numbers using multiplication that shows equivalent quantities; for example, $(2 \times 3) \times 4 = 2 \times (3 \times 4)$.

authentic assessment   The concept of model, practice, and feedback in which students know what excellent performance is and are guided to practice an entire concept rather than bits and pieces in preparation for eventual understanding.

bay A body of water that is a part of a sea or an ocean. It is partly enclosed by land.

benchmark A standard by which student performance can be measured in order to compare it with and improve one's own skills or learning.

Bloom's taxonomy A classification system for learning objectives that consists of six levels ranging from knowledge (which focuses on the reproduction of facts) to evaluation (which represents higher-level thinking).

bluff The high, steep side of a rock or the earth.

canyon A deep, narrow valley with steep sides.

cardinal directions The four main compass directions: north, south, east, and west.

carnivores Organisms (consumers) that eat animals.

cartographer A person who makes maps.

circuit tester An instrument used to determine if electrical current is flowing in a series or parallel circuit.

cliff The high, steep side of a rock or the earth.

coast Land along a sea or an ocean.

compass rose A symbol on a map that shows the directions.

competency test A test intended to determine whether a student has met established minimum standards of skills and knowledge and is thus eligible for promotion, graduation, certification, or other official acknowledgment of achievement.

comprehension The understanding of what you have read.

concept An abstract, general notion—a heading that characterizes a set of behaviors and beliefs.

conductor A substance or medium that conducts heat, light, sound, or especially an electric charge.

cone A three-dimensional shape that has a circle for a base and a curved surface, and comes to a point at the top.

congruency Two quantities that correspond; having the same size and shape.

congruent   Shapes that have the same size and shape.

conjunction   A word such as "and," "or," and "but" that connects other words, ideas, phrases, clauses, and sentences.

consumers   Organisms that rely on other organisms as food sources.

content goals   Statements that are like learning standards or learning objectives, but which only describe the topics to be studied, not the skills to be performed.

contraction   A word or a phrase that is formed by leaving out one or more letters or combining some of the sounds of a longer phrase.

coordinate graph   A device for locating points in a plane by using ordered pairs of numbers. The graph is formed by the intersection of two number lines. The intersection forms right angles.

coordinate graphing   A graph of any system of numbers used to find the position of a point.

criterion-referenced test   A test in which the results can be used to determine a student's progress toward mastery of a content area or designated objectives of an instructional program. Performance is compared to an expected level of mastery in a content area rather than to other students' scores.

cube   A three-dimensional shape with six square faces.

curriculum   The content and skills that are taught at each grade level.

curriculum alignment   The connection of subjects across grade levels, cumulatively, to build comprehensive, increasingly complex instructional programs.

cylinder   A three-dimensional shape that has a curved surface and a parallel, congruent, circular, or elliptical base.

decimal   A quantity less than a whole, expressed with a point, based on the number ten.

denominator   The bottom number of a fraction. It represents the number of equal parts into which the object has been broken.

desert   An area of dry land without many plants.

developmental delay　When a child is developing skills that only come with emotional and intellectual growth more slowly than other students.

developmental disorder　When a child is developing skills that only come with emotional and intellectual growth more slowly than other students, not developing those developmental skills at all, or not developing those skills normally.

difference　The answer you get when you subtract one number from another.

direct object　A noun or a pronoun that is having an action done to it.

dividend　The number that is being divided in a division problem.

divisor　The number that divides another number in a division problem.

elapsed time　The amount of time that has passed while some event is happening.

elevation　The height of land.

equator　An imaginary line that divides the earth into the northern hemisphere and the southern hemisphere.

equivalent　Equal in amount or value.

erosion　The act of wearing away material from the earth's surface by weathering or other things (such as human use).

estimate　An approximate amount or value.

fact families　Show how addition and subtraction as well as multiplication and division are related.

fluency　The ability to read quickly and effortlessly.

fossil　A remnant or trace of an organism of a past geologic age, such as a skeleton or a leaf imprint, embedded and preserved in the earth's crust.

fraction　A quantity less than a whole, expressed as a quotient of two quantities.

genetic predisposition　An inherited genetic pattern that makes one susceptible to a certain characteristic.

genre   A type of literary work.

graphic organizer   An aid to organize information in order to remember and understand the information.

grid   A pattern of regularly spaced horizontal and vertical lines forming squares on a map or a chart that can be used as a reference for locating points.

gulf   A large body of water that is partly enclosed by land.

habitat   The place where an organism usually lives.

harbor   An area of water where ships can dock.

hemisphere   Either the northern or southern half of the earth as divided by the equator, or the eastern or western half of the earth as divided by the prime meridian.

herbivores   Organisms (consumers) that eat plants.

high-stakes testing   Any testing program whose results have important consequences for students, teachers, colleges, and/or areas, such as promotion, certification, graduation, or denial/approval of services and opportunity.

hill   Land that is taller than the land around it.

homonyms   Words that sound the same but have different meanings. The words can be spelled the same or have different spellings.

hundreds chart   A 10×10 grid that has 100 boxes in which the numbers 1 through 100 are written, one number per box.

hypothesis   A proposed explanation for an observation, phenomenon, or scientific problem that can be tested by further investigation.

indirect object   A noun or pronoun that tells you for what or whom the action of the verb (predicate) is being done.

inherited traits   Behaviors that are passed from parent to offspring through the genes.

insulator   A material that protects, especially from sound, heat, or electricity.

interjection   An exclamation or utterance, such as "wow!" "oh," or "huh."

intermediate directions   The directions between the cardinal directions. They include northeast, northwest, southeast, and southwest.

intersecting lines   Lines that cross or overlap.

IQ test   A psychometric test that scores the performance of certain intellectual tasks and can provide assessors with a measurement of general intelligence.

island   Land that is completely surrounded by water.

lake   A body of water that is surrounded by land.

learned traits   Behaviors that are taught.

learning disability   The inability to learn in the same way or at the same pace as other students. Developmental skills needed at this age are either missing or hyperdeveloped.

learning objectives   A set of expectations that are needed to meet the learning standard.

learning standards   Broad statements that describe what content a student should know and what skills a student should be able to demonstrate in different subject areas.

mass   A property of matter equal to the measure of an object's resistance to change in either the speed or direction of its motion. The mass of an object is not dependent on gravity and therefore is different from but proportional to its weight.

measurement   Quantitative description of student learning and qualitative description of student attitude.

median   The point on a scale that divides a group into two equal subgroups. The median is not affected by low or high scores as is the mean. (See also **norm**.)

metacognition   The knowledge of one's own thinking processes and strategies, and the ability to consciously reflect and act on the knowledge of cognition to modify those processes and strategies.

molecule   The smallest particle of a substance that retains the chemical and physical properties of the substance and is composed of two or more atoms; a group of like or different atoms held together by chemical forces.

mountain   The tallest type of landform.

multiple   A number that may be divided by another number with no remainder.

multiple-choice test   A test in which students are presented with a question or an incomplete sentence or idea. The students are expected to choose the correct or best answer or completion from a menu of alternatives.

nonequivalent   Not equal in amount or value.

norm   A distribution of scores obtained from a norm group. The norm is the midpoint (or median) of scores or performance of the students in that group. Fifty percent will score above the norm and 50 percent will score below it.

norm group   A random group of students selected by a test developer to take a test to provide a range of scores and establish the percentiles of performance for use in determining scoring standards.

norm-referenced test   A test in which a student or a group's performance is compared to that of a norm group. The results are relative to the performance of an external group and are designed to be compared with the norm group, resulting in a performance standard. These tests are often used to measure and compare students, schools, districts, and states on the basis of norm-established scales of achievement.

noun   Names a person, place, thing, feeling, idea, or act.

obtuse angle   An angle that is greater than 90°.

ocean   A large body of salt water.

organism   An individual form of life, such as a plant or an animal.

outcome   An operationally defined educational goal, usually a culminating activity, product, or performance that can be measured.

parallel lines   Lines that never intersect or cross and are the same distance apart at all points of the line.

peninsula   Land that is almost completely surrounded by water.

performance-based assessment　Direct observation and rating of student performance of an educational objective, often an ongoing observation over a period of time, and typically involving the creation of products dealing with real life. Performance-based assessments use performance criteria to determine the degree to which a student has met an achievement target. Important elements of performance-based assessment include clear goals or performance criteria clearly articulated and communicated to the learner.

performance goals　Statements that are like learning standards or learning objectives but they only describe the skills to be performed, not the content to be studied.

perimeter　The distance around a closed figure.

permutations　The changing of the elements in a set.

perpendicular lines　Lines that intersect or cross to form four right angles.

place savers　Zeros that are placed when multiplying two-digit numbers or larger; for example, the tens column equals 1 zero, the hundreds column equals 2 zeros, and so on.

place value　The value of a digit depending on its place in a number.

plain　A large area of flat land.

plateau　An area of high, flat land with steep sides.

plural noun　A noun that refers to two or more people, places, or things.

polygon　A closed plane figure bounded by three or more line segments.

portfolio assessment　A systematic and organized collection of a student's work that exhibits to others the direct evidence of a student's efforts, achievements, and progress over a period of time. The collection should involve the student in selection of its contents and should include information about the performance criteria, the rubric or criteria for judging merit, and evidence of student self-relocation or evaluation. It should include representative work, providing documentation of the learner's performance and a basis for evaluation of the student's progress. Portfolios may include a variety of demonstrations of learning.

predicate   A verb that describes what the noun (subject) of a sentence is doing or being.

preposition   A word that shows the relationship between one noun and a different noun, verb, or adverb, such as "in" or "through."

prime meridian   An imaginary line that divides the earth into the eastern hemisphere and the western hemisphere.

probability   The chance that a particular outcome will occur, measured as a ratio of the total of possible outcomes.

producers   Organisms that create their own food.

product   The answer you get when you multiply two numbers.

product map   A map that shows the various products in a state or region.

pronoun   A word that replaces a noun, such as "he," "they," or "it."

proper noun   The name of a particular person, place, or thing; it begins with a capital letter.

properties   A characteristic attribute possessed by all members of a class.

pyramid   A three-dimensional shape in which one face is some type of polygon and all of the other faces are triangles.

quotient   An answer to a division problem.

random outcomes   Outcomes that no one can predict and only happen by chance, such as the flip of a coin, the roll of a number cube, or the spin of a spinner.

rectangular coordinate system   A graph of any system of numbers used to find the position of a point.

rectangular prism   A prism whose faces, including the base, are all rectangles.

regrouping   A process used in subtraction. You might have to regroup from one place-value position to another in order to have enough to subtract from each place-value position. For example, you might need to take 1 ten from the tens position and regroup it as 10 ones in the ones position.

right angle   An angle that equals 90°.

river   A large stream of water that flows across the land.

rounding   A type of estimation. For example, if you round 230 to the nearest hundred, you ask yourself whether the number is closer to 200 or 300. The answer is 200.

scale   A standard of measurement or judgment; a criterion.

scientific method   The principles and procedures of discovery and demonstration that are necessary for a scientific experiment.

sea   A body of salt water that is smaller than an ocean.

sedimentation   A deposition of a material such as soil or sand by mechanical means from a state of suspension from air or water.

serial order   An order of organization or a hierarchy, in which each element is graded or ranked (like an inverted tree structure).

shore   The land along the edge of an ocean, sea, lake, or river.

singular noun   A word that refers to one person, place, or thing.

solid   Having a definite shape and volume.

spatial reasoning   The ability to describe, understand, and conceptualize the position and orientation of objects in three-dimensional shapes.

sphere   A three-dimensional shape that has a curved surface with all points a given distance from its center point. A ball is an example of a sphere.

statistics   A number value, such as the mean that characterizes the sample from which it came.

strait   A narrow channel of water that connects two larger bodies of water.

subject   A noun or pronoun that is performing the verb; the "doer" of a sentence.

subsystem   A part of a larger system that works together to make the whole system function.

sum   The answer you get when you add.

summary   Telling the main ideas or events.

swamp   An area of low, wet land with trees.

symmetry   When an object or shape is divided in half, both sides are exactly the same.

synonym   A word that means the same thing as another word.

system   A group of interacting elements that forms a whole.

tally   To count or keep a record.

topographic map   A map with detailed and raised areas that shows the shape of the surface of the land.

tributary   A stream or river that empties into a larger river.

valley   An area of low land between hills or mountains.

variable   A letter representing any unknown number.

Venn diagram   A diagram that is made up of two or more overlapping circles, often used in mathematics to show relationships between sets.

verb   A word that describes an action.

verb tense   A part of speech that tells you when the action happened. The main forms are present (I sing), past (I sang), future (I will sing), present participle (I am singing), and past participle (I have sung).

volcano   An opening in the earth through which lava, rock, ashes, and gases are forced out.

volume   The amount of space occupied in three dimensions: length, width, and height.

weathering   To discolor, disintegrate, wear, or otherwise affect something adversely by exposure.

BIBLIOGRAPHY

Bloom, B. S. (ed.) (1956). *Taxonomy of Educational Objectives: The Classification of Educational Goals: Handbook I, Cognitive Domain.* New York: Longmans, Green.

Brainerd, C. J. (1978). *Piaget's Theory of Intelligence.* New Jersey: Prentice Hall, Inc.

Evans, R. (1973). *Jean Piaget: The Man and His Ideas.* New York: E. P. Dutton & Co., Inc.

Lavatelli, C. (1973). *Piaget's Theory Applied to an Early Childhood Curriculum.* Boston: American Science and Engineering, Inc.

London, C. (1988). "A Piagetian constructivist perspective on curriculum development." *Reading Improvement 27,* 82–95.

Piaget, J. (1972). "Development and Learning." In Lavatelli, C. S., and Stendler, F. *Reading in Child Behavior and Development.* New York: Harcourt Brace Janovich.

——— (1972). *To Understand Is to Invent.* New York: The Viking Press, Inc.

Shure, M. B. (1993). *Interpersonal Problem Solving and Prevention: A Comprehensive Report of Research and Training.* A five-year longitudinal study, Kindergarten through grade 4, no. MH-40801. Washington, D.C.: National Institute of Mental Health.

Shure, M. B., and G. Spivack (1980). "Interpersonal Problem Solving as a Mediator of Behavioral Adjustment in Preschool and Kindergarten Children." *Journal of Applied Developmental Psychology 1* 29–44.

——— (1982). "Interpersonal Problem-solving in Young Children: A Cognitive Approach to Prevention." *American Journal of Community Psychology 10,* 341–356.

Sigel, I., and R. Cocking (1977). *Cognitive Development from Childhood to Adolescence: A Constructivist Perspective.* New York: Holt, Rinehart and Winston.

Singer, D., and T. Revenson (1978). *A Piaget Primer: How a Child Thinks.* New York: International Universities Press, Inc.

Willis, Mariaemma, and Victoria Hodson (1999). *Discover Your Child's Learning Style.* New York: Crown Publishing Group.

INDEX